ABOUT THE AUTHOR

John Cornelius was born in 1949 and studied Fine Art at Liverpool College of Art. Although he mainly works as an art teacher and freelance writer, he has had a variety of jobs including songwriter and rock musician. Much of the material in this book was drawn from his experiences as a quick-sketch portrait-artist, working in and around the late-drinking clubs of Liverpool 8. He wrote *The City of Liverpool Guide Book* (1985), and he has contributed poetry and illustrations to a number of anthologies including *A Bit of England* (with Dave Hall, 1985), *Jewels and Binoculars* (Stride, 1993), and *Things We Said Today* (poems about the Beatles, Stride, 1995). His journalism has appeared in newspapers and magazines ranging from *The Guardian* and *New Society* to *Practical Fishkeeping*. He is married with three stepsons.

JOHN CORNELIUS

Liverpool 8

Illustrated by the author

LIVERPOOL UNIVERSITY PRESS

First published 1982 by
John Murray (Publishers) Limited

Reprinted 2001 by
Liverpool University Press
4 Cambridge Street
Liverpool L69 7ZU

British Library Cataloguing-in-Publication data
A British Library CIP record is available

ISBN 0-85323-877-4

Printed and bound in the European Union by
Bookcraft Ltd, Midsomer Norton, Somerset

CONTENTS

PREFACE TO REPRINT EDITION

LIVERPOOL 8, the book, is, as I write, 19 years old. Past the age of majority. It can now leave home, go out into the world and earn its keep. Some of the tales in it are 30 or more years old. As for Liverpool 8 the place, I no longer live there and only have hearsay evidence to go on as to how it's changed. The remit for this preface was to make a link between then and now. I'm not sure of the relevance of temporal change: I always maintained that Liverpool 8 was not so much a place as a state of mind; an unpunctuated state of mind that wrapped up the pubs the shops the art college the cathedral the early mornings the late nights the dawn chorus the clubs the police vans the architecture the poets the musicians the prostitutes the students the semi-famous the famous the down and out the luxurious tasteful homes of the successful the seedy bedsits of the failures the has-beens and the never-will-bes the people who just live and work there the vegetarians the alcoholics the shallow poseurs the stunning geniuses who never got a chance the microtalents who got all the chances the godlike peaceful ones the psychos the great painters the conmen the rhinestone cowboys the real cowboys the indians the sycamores the hawthorns the marbletop tables with the castiron lion legs the gilt mirrors the stuffed owls the teabags the instant coffee the catshit the grimy staircases the love the life the death into one cerebral parcel.

In a moment of optimism and blindness to some of what was happening around me, and indeed to me, I ended the book with the sweeping statement, 'life is good.' I should have added: ' – when you compare it with the alternative.'

In retrospect, some bits of the book are patronising and politically incorrect; some bits go too far; other bits don't go far enough; some make me cringe; others still make me laugh. There are people mentioned who, if I hadn't fossilised them in print, would have long vacated my memory. Others, great ones who meant a lot to me, didn't get a mention. After publication, some wanted to shake my hand and buy me a pint; others in the mistaken belief that having a book out brings instant wealth, expected me to do all the buying. Still others wanted to push my face in or sue me. People who had ignored me went out of their way to catch my attention. People who had always greeted me warmly became wary. Puritans thought the book decadent. Some said that racists and reactionaries thought I was a trendy lefty. Others said that trendy lefties thought I was a racist and reactionary. Political types thought I was naive. Naive types thought I was political. Arty farties thought I wrote too much about ordinary people. Ordinary people thought I wrote too much about arty farties. What a mess: I just thought it was good clean fun.

The book was reviewed in the South China Sea Morning Post, the Dublin Sunday Press and the South African Rand Daily News. It was ignored by the *Liverpool Echo*. W. H.

Smith in Church Street said it was the most stolen book they had. Or didn't have any more. Philip Son and Nephew in Whitechapel devoted a whole window to stacks of copies. I remember one wet miserable day, when I didn't even have the price of a packet of fags in my pocket, gazing bleakly into the shop window while a huge poster of myself grinned stupidly back at me. Many people told me they loved the book and couldn't put it down; others read it over and over and then started pulling it to bits.

The book came out the way it did because of my state of mind then. A year later, or a year earlier, I would have written a completely different book with the same title. I could have written a different book every year with the same title. Some writers write the same book over and over again but with a different title, always trying to make the same point but never quite crystallising it.

So here it is. New edition, old book; timeless place. Same point.

John Cornelius
London, July 2001

ACKNOWLEDGEMENTS

I would like to thank the following for allowing me to work on their premises: Messrs Erik and David Moore; Mr 'Dutch' Eddy and all of the staff at the Tudor Club; Abdul and his staff at the Alahram Club. And my thanks, of course, to the citizens of Liverpool 8 and to the many hundreds of night-owls from all corners of the globe, who, over the years, have allowed me the privilege and the pleasure of sketching their portraits. This book is for you, because without you it never would have been written. Finally, the biggest thank you of all to my wife, Pam, who was obliged to sit at home night after night while I was out gathering material for *Liverpool 8*, though neither of us realised it at the time.

J.C.

A Local Correspondent

Liverpool 8 equals Toxteth equals riots. Equals trouble, in other words. Or so you'd think if you took the media reports as gospel.

When I started work on this book in June 1981, Liverpool 8 was an officially redundant term for a particular postal district on Merseyside. That's all it was. If you live here, as I do, your correct postcode is now Liverpool L8 XYZ2 or whatever. But the inhabitants still insist on referring to the place as Liverpool 8. Part of the area is also called Dingle. But the 'official' name for most of it is Toxteth, a word of Roman origin – a word which, again, local people rarely use, despite the fact that at the junction of Princes Avenue and Upper Parliament Street there is a sign which says: City of Liverpool – Toxteth.

So the idea of the book was to try and give a personal impression of an earthy, colourful district which would show the reader facets of Liverpool 8 which the media tended to ignore. To an outsider, if he'd heard anything of Liverpool 8 at all it was of a multiracial, social-deprivation area. A 'problem' area. Which is true, of course – up to a point. One or two slightly better informed observers may have been aware of other aspects of life in Liverpool 8, such as its small artists' quarter or its rather grandiose architecture; all of which is fascinating, if perhaps a little low-key for sub-editors.

Then, without warning, a month later – 5/6 July 1981 – Liverpool 8 exploded. Newspapers the world over carried stark pictures of my local off-licence and fishmonger's shop burning down. A nearby furniture warehouse blazed brightly on the cover of an international glossy news magazine. It was a bizarre experience, out shopping, having to fight one's way through an entire American film-crew blocking the doorway of the greengrocer's.

Toxteth? Riots. Riots? Toxteth. The words – like Brixton in London or St Paul's in Bristol – have become almost interchangeable. Though this is not the place to discuss the reasons for the astounding events of that hot, tense summer, most people who live in the area, though stunned and frightened, were not surprised at what took place. The real wonder was that it hadn't happened earlier. Certainly, it is an appalling thing to see young policemen being led off into ambulances, blood gushing from horrendous head-wounds. It was tragic to see so many familiar landmarks destroyed in a couple of nightmare orgies of burning and looting. But it has to be said: if you keep on pestering a dog, no matter how good-humoured he is, sooner or later he's going to turn around and bite. And once he starts biting, the memory of all the flicks and kicks he's ever received will come welling up. So he'll bite, bite and bite again.

Liverpool 8 has been kicked unmercifully; yet it remains a faithful hound. One night during the troubles a youth was killed by a police vehicle. Soon the people of Toxteth were on the streets again. To fight? Not this time. To celebrate the Royal Wedding.

Toxteth is by no means the grimmest area of Liverpool. There are worse places, in my view. Edge Hill, Scotland-Exchange, Speke, Vauxhall, parts of Wavertree, Everton and Anfield share some of our area's worst aspects – slums, dereliction, unemployment, crime and high-rise, prison-like dwellings – with little of the character and colour which helps, to some extent, to counteract these things in Liverpool 8. Then, of course, farther out of town there is mile after mile of semi-detached suburbia – zones which contain the lower-middle-class ennui that paralyses many a provincial city; the buffer that ensures that nothing ever changes. It was in such an area that I grew up – Crosby, scene of the SDP/Liberal Alliance's historic victory in 1981 – though I was born within shouting distance of Gladstone Dock and escaped suburban

'Character and colour survive in the slums'

strangulation for at least the first ten years of life. It is probably for these reasons that the variety and vigour of Liverpool 8 has made such a deep impression on me: not only did the place offer a complete contrast to the bland suburban adolescence, it reawakened my recognition of my own working-class, dock-land roots.

My contact with Liverpool 8 began about fifteen years ago: as a would-be art student, then as a real art student, then as an art school dropout, rock musician, sometime poet, old-fashioned street artist and workaday family person. Except that I didn't really drop out of art college. I completed the course but refused to write the kind of stiff, academic disser-tation that you had to produce to obtain a degree in art. Consequently, they refused to part with my degree until I'd written this ten thousand-word essay in the required style – or, rather, non-style. Which I did, however, in moments of self-doubt, eight years later. Eventually, my degree arrived, rolled up in a cardboard tube.

The odd thing is, that before this tube arrived, jobs such as teaching were out of my reach, even though now I've got it nobody wants to see it. This was lucky in a way. Because, although for a long time I was struggling to keep not only my own body and soul together but also those of a wife and kids, the fact that I needed to be able to buy food and pay bills meant that I had to go out onto the streets of Liverpool 8 and find some way of earning a living. I took stock of my situation and thought, now what can I do? What abilities do I have that can be turned into bread and wine? The list was very brief, although there was a lot of things I *couldn't* do. I couldn't be a window-cleaner, for example, because I've got a game leg and can't climb ladders; also I've got this fear of heights. There must be something wrong with at least half of my brain – the half that normally does things such as wiring up an electric plug or plumbing in a wash-basin or knocking a nail into a wall in such a way that it doesn't bend in fourteen different directions. Or driving a car. I mean, any bloody idiot can drive a car. The streets of Liverpool are full of them, careering about

4

'A priest from the West African Pentecostal Church takes a walk down Canning Street'

'A derelict hotel on Princes Avenue'

the place, scattering artists in all directions. Not me, though. I can't drive a car. My Dad did try, once, to give me lessons on Seaforth Sands. Luckily there was a group of lads nearby playing football, who helped us to dig the car out of the sand. Even some of the things I could do quite efficiently were of no use when it came to making money; so the list became even shorter. For example, I was quite good at writing songs. I could play the guitar, after a fashion. Also sing a bit. But they just laughed at me, down at the Labour Exchange, when I mentioned this.

'Nothing in that line today. Try Friday. In the meantime, why don't you register as a labourer?'

All things considered, the only thing left on the list was art. Even this didn't seem too promising. I got a series of jobs as a commercial artist – a graphic designer. One job was in an advertising agency and was, well, boring. 'Artist', indeed. All

'Windsor Street'

you did was draw straight lines with a ruler (I wasn't very good at this, either) and paste pieces of paper together to make up advertisements for local newspapers. If a job cropped up that required an illustration, they wouldn't give it to me to do. They'd give it to this bloke who'd been working there for about twenty years. He couldn't draw to save his life, but he'd carefully trace around a photograph of a car or a washing machine or a bottle of deodorant and stick this transparent stuff with dots on all over it so that the finished results looked very professional. It fooled nearly everybody. Another job I had was making and painting the scenery for the Christmas Grotto in a department store. This job could have been OK except that you had to stick rigidly to designs which had been drawn up fifty years previously and were considered sacred and not to be altered. Consequently the whole thing was a bit like painting by numbers and was no more creative than slapping a coat of paint on a front door.

No matter what nonsensical job I was doing during the day, at night I was hanging about the clubs and dives of Liverpool 8 sketching portraits to make a few bob. And these places were where I plugged into the mainstream of life which was passing me by during the day. This was why I now consider myself lucky that the cardboard tube hadn't arrived earlier. With a safe, comfortable teaching job, for example, I may never have hit the streets with my sketch-pad, and this book, at least in its present form, may never have been written.

There's always something new to look at in Liverpool 8, whether it's a sagging house that wasn't sagging yesterday or some odd character you've never noticed before, such as the elderly man in the woollen bobble-hat, often to be seen down Lodge Lane, who habitually wears his jacket *outside* his macintosh. Walk down Park Road, Princes Avenue, Lodge Lane, Canning Street, Catharine Street, Granby Street, Mulgrave Street, Parliament Street, Huskisson Street or Falkner Square and you can bet your life you'll see something or someone out of the ordinary. To an artist or to a writer the place is a gift. Can't think of anything to paint? Just glance out of the

'The iron bridge and Fairy Glen, Sefton Park'

window. A blank page taunting you from the typewriter? Take a walk down the street. If you can't find *anything* to spark you off out there, you're probably in the wrong business.

Strolling around the slum areas – Sussex Gardens, Kent Street, Windsor Street and thereabouts – it is a pungent irony that wherever you happen to be, the giant figure of the Anglican Cathedral is towering above the rooftops. Built in a modern Gothic style its distinctive head-and-shoulders shape and the odd way in which it appears to alter its dimensions according to your viewpoint make it an eerie but inescapable fixture of the Liverpool skyline. Sometimes it appears to be way over in the distance; other times it looms suddenly huge as you turn a corner. But wherever you are in Liverpool 8, the Cathedral is only a mile away at most. While the building of this gargantuan structure provided employment for generations of Irish Liverpudlians, its dramatically landscaped cemetery has, for almost as long, provided a summer retreat for hordes of children, old people, unwanted cats and dogs and dope-smoking individuals on the fringes of society, looking for a safe, sunny refuge on hot summer days. If you want the best possible view of the Anglican Cathedral (the distinction is important: there's the Roman Catholic Cathedral at the opposite end of Hope Street) rent a flat in Gambier Terrace, over the way. But not if you happen to suffer from migraine: the bells ring loud and clear.

Some of the stories in *Liverpool 8* arise from my memories of that crazy period in the sixties when half the world seemed to be decked out in flowers, beads, caftans and sandals; some stem from the tired, worn-out aftermath that was the seventies; some are happening now, in the eighties. But in a strange way they all strive to tell the truth about this one small area of a once-great international port, now a provincial city, which seems to be running rapidly out of steam. *Liverpool 8* is not an autobiography; it is an attempt at a biography of an area which, in my view, can be regarded as not just an oddball postal district but a bastion of individuality.

'There's an old piano and they play it hot behind the green door'

1 *The Green Door Mystery*

'Green door, what's that secret you're keeping?' I always wondered what went on behind that green door. One night – one fateful night – I found out.

The Green Door Mystery goes back a long way. I must have been, what, ten? Twelve? I don't know, pretty young, anyway. Round at this other kid's house. He lived on a council estate but his mother reckoned she was a cut above the neighbours because she was paying for the house. Not renting it, like everyone else. This kid, Eccles, was a spoilt brat. Had everything he ever wanted. An only child, his Dad was a sailor. In those days, lots of kids' Dads were sailors. Away for months, even a year or more, then all of a sudden coming home like a conquering hero, laden with presents. Smelling-

13

things for the Mum, African masks, bamboo whistles that didn't whistle, all packed into that long bag slung over the shoulder. Slamming taxi doors hard, dashing the driver a fiver. Very impressive. And loads of money! Eccles always had a couple of quid. In those days that was big money. This complete stranger he called Dad would buy loads of whisky, spend a lot of time in bed for a few weeks and then off . . . off again.

To me and my friend Batstooth, with Dads permanently installed at home, all this was a puzzle. Our Dads would disappear at eight o'clock in the morning, sure enough. But somehow they always managed to be back home round about tea-time, feet up in front of the fire, dozing in front of the TV. The telly was quite a recent invention at that time, or at least not many people had one, ordinary people that is. Eccles had one. So did I, so did Batstooth. Tiny ones, nine-inch glowing green screen, the first primitive advertising jingles chirping tinnily:

'Did you Maclean your teeth today?'

'You'll wonder where the yellow went,
When you brush your teeth with Pepsodent!'

'THE COLGATE INVISIBLE SHIELD,' a man would announce sternly. It seemed to be all teeth in those days. Even the pop singers, with legs like columns of syrup poured from a can, had shiny teeth. Tommy Steele, Cliff Richard.

Eccles's telly, of course, had an eighteen-inch screen. Twice as big as everyone else's. One rainy afternoon, Batstooth and I called on Eccles. Strangely enough, Eccles's front door wasn't green. All the houses on the block were identical, painted Corporation green. Green window frames, green gutters, green drainpipes. And a green door. Eccles's door, however, was yellow. Because Eccles's Mum and occasional Dad were buying the house on a mortgage, they had complete artistic control over it. This meant that they could paint the front door whatever the hell colour they liked. For a long time, I thought that a mortgage, as opposed to rent, meant exactly this.

14

So, while most Dads were content to spend their weekends in white Bri-Nylon shirts that you could see the string vest through and baggy, biscuit-coloured weekend trousers, mowing the grass, Eccles's Dad would appear spasmodically, home from Hong Kong or somewhere, come three thousand miles just to paint this front door a different colour. Any colour, just so long as it wasn't green like all the others. No point in buying a house if you're going to paint it the same colour as everyone else's. Having painted the door and drunk some whisky, he'd go back to Hong Kong for some more bamboo whistles.

Like I said, the particular day Batstooth and I called on Eccles, the front door was yellow. We knocked on it and Eccles opened up. He was on his own, as usual. This was another funny thing about Eccles. His mother was never in. She would leave him a fiver, 'Just in case . . .', then disappear for hours and hours. Eccles didn't mind. He was used to it.

Something else strange about Eccles's house. The toilet was in the back kitchen, instead of upstairs. That's right, believe it or not. To the right of the kitchen door was a cupboard. But when you opened it, there was a toilet. Two other things were unusual about this. The cistern, instead of being right up in the air with a chain hanging down with a wooden thing on the end, was low down, just behind the toilet and instead of having a chain, it had a handle! That's the truth, a handle! But not only that. The other peculiar thing was that the bath was in the same room as the toilet! This, in my opinion – and Batstooth agreed – was going too far. What happened if, for example, you wanted to go to the toilet when someone was in the bath? Did you have to wait till they'd finished in the bath, or did they have to get out of the bath, dripping wet, and stand in the kitchen while you went for a pee. And supposing you wanted to do something stronger than a pee. Did the other person, freezing cold, wet and dripping, have to get back in the bath with that terrible stink still in the air?

Eccles, however, had a simple answer to all this. You're never going to believe this, not in a million years. Eccles had – are you ready for this? – *two toilets*! No, we didn't believe it either. But he did have. Out there in the back yard was a small shed containing another toilet. An ordinary one, this time, with a chain and everything. But unusually clean and white, for an outside toilet. There was even a lightbulb that you could switch on. Anyone who's been to an outside toilet, full of spiders, in the dark, at night, will know what an advantage this lightbulb would have been.

But as it happened, and Eccles also pointed this out, he was on his own in the house so much that all of this talk about the bath and the toilet was academic. The truth was, he could use either toilet at any time without interruption. And the kitchen toilet had the supreme advantage that if, say, Eccles was in the bath and suddenly wanted to go to the toilet, all he had to do was step out of the bath and sit on the toilet. This certainly seemed a big plus to Batstooth and myself. We had to admit it: you just couldn't go wrong in Eccles's house where toilets were concerned. As if all of this wasn't enough, Eccles told us something else. Although he hadn't made use of this himself, he'd seen his Dad on odd occasions demonstrating yet another advantage of this close proximity between bath and toilet: you

could sit on the toilet and be sick into the bath at the same time! Apparently, Eccles had come downstairs one night for a drink of water and was surprised to find the toilet door open and the light on. He looked inside and there was his Dad, pyjama pants around his ankles, doing a poo (diarrhoea, Eccles reckoned), sitting on the toilet. Both taps were switched on and roaring away and Eccles's Dad was leaning over, saying 'Never again' and being sick into the bath. Eccles had wanted to find out how he managed to do all this without making any mess on the floor but his Dad told him to go away. After this, whenever his Dad was home, Eccles often came down in the night to watch him doing this.

Another thing about Eccles's house, though this was nothing to do with the mortgage or the toilets, was the smell of burning which always seemed to be in the air. This was because of Eccles being on his own all the time. And this day we called, Batstooth and I, the day the front door was yellow, there was a very strong smell of burning. It turned out to be because of this electric guitar that Eccles's Dad had brought home for Eccles once. It was the strangest looking instrument you've ever seen. I've never seen one like it since. It had an almost circular body and a wooden neck. And the body was made of metal. Eccles couldn't play it, of course. But he found other uses for it. The guitar was shaped rather like a frying-pan. And on this occasion it was the cause of the burning smell.

Eccles had placed about half a dozen pieces of bacon on the guitar, on the round part, across the strings, and had shuffled it about above the lighted gas-ring on the cooker, just like a frying-pan. He was in the middle of this when we called. While he was coming to answer the door, he put the guitar down on the gas-ring and some of the bacon must have caught fire. Anyway, when we got into the kitchen, there was this terrible smell of burning and black smoke rising. And the wooden handle or neck had also seemed to have caught fire. Eccles picked it up and ran into the bathroom, plunging the whole thing under the hot water tap, gushing and steaming.

17

I forgot to mention that the bathroom door was green. This is important. Even though the front door was yellow, the bathroom door was green. Eccles left the guitar hissing and steaming away in the bathroom, the burning smell now coming from there instead of from the cooker, although bits of the cooker were still smoking a little. We decided to put some records on his mother's record-player. Of course, the record-player wasn't a little green Dansette with a hole kicked in the speaker where his mother had tripped over it, like mine was. Eccles's mother's record-player was a big, wooden, polished stereogram thing with a cupboard where all the records were kept. We had a look through the record collection. Most of it was rubbish. LPs like *Carousel* and *South Pacific*. *South Pacific* didn't sound too bad played at 78 rpm, especially 'There is Nothing like a Dame' which sounded great at that speed. Suddenly, Batstooth came across a small record, a 45, and waved it about.

'This is a good one,' he said.

I took it off him and had a look. It was by a man named

Frankie Vaughan. I didn't know it then, but Frankie Vaughan lived in Liverpool 8. The name of the record was 'Green Door'. It had a green label, too. On close examination, I noticed that there was a bit of toffee or something stuck into the grooves of the record, right near the end where the smooth part starts, before it goes into the label.

'All right, let's play it then.'

We placed it on the turntable, at the right speed. If it turned out to be no good, we'd put it on at a different speed. It crackled a bit, then it started playing.

I'll tell you something, that 'Green Door' was a good record. It had a story to it. I'd always liked songs with stories to them, like 'Davy Crocket, King of the Wild Frontier', that kind of record. This particular story was about this man wondering what was going on behind this green door. This Frankie Vaughan man was sitting in his house and there was a green door somewhere, like the one on Eccles's toilet, and he was wondering what was going on behind it and no one would tell him. Maybe someone was sitting on the toilet, being sick into the bath, like Eccles's Dad, and this Frankie Vaughan had come down for a drink of water to see what was going on . . . wait a minute, what's he singing . . .?

'. . . there's an old piano and they play it hot behind the Green Door . . .'

Hey, that was just like Eccles's guitar, smouldering away in the bathroom! Only this bathroom Frankie Vaughan was singing about had a hot piano in it, instead of a hot guitar.

Right at the end of the song, a piano went 'bink-bonk' and Frankie Vaughan sang quietly, '. . . Green Door, what's that secret you're keeping?' and then he sang louder, nearly shouting: 'Green Door!' and the drums and the band went 'bomp-bomp' and there the record ended. Or there it was supposed to end, but Eccles's Mum's copy of the record had that piece of toffee stuck in it and instead of the record ending, the needle jumped back to where the piano went 'bink-bonk' and played the ending all over again. Whispering: '. . . Green Door, what's that secret you're keeping . . .?' Shouting: 'Green

19

Door!' Bomp-bomp. And it played this ending over and over again.

Meanwhile, Eccles had gone back into the bathroom to see how the guitar was getting on. While he was in there, Batstooth and I had this great idea. Another distinctive thing about Eccles's toilet door was that there was a bolt on it, on the outside. Batstooth and I couldn't see the sense in this at first. A lock on the *inside*, certainly, to stop people blundering in while you were on the toilet or being sick in the bath or something. But not on the *outside*.

Of course, as ever, there was a perfectly sound reason for the lock on the toilet door in Eccles's house to be on the outside, instead of the inside like everyone else's. This, explained Eccles, was to stop burglars getting in. Before his Mum went to bed at night, she would lock the toilet door from the outside, so that if a burglar got in through the toilet window, he couldn't get any further. He'd have to either stay in the toilet or climb back out again. And with the kind of thing that went on in Eccles's toilet, sick, diarrhoea and burning guitars and all that, it was most unlikely that he would want to stay long. Although we supposed that he might make off with that Mickey Mouse jug thing with Eccles's toothbrush in it or the small razor that – so Eccles claimed – his Mum shaved her legs with. Once again, the steamrollering logic of the Eccles household had floored us.

Actually, Batstooth and I were getting a little bit cheesed off with the smart-Alec, slick reasons for all these unusual things in Eccles's house. While he was in the toilet sorting the guitar out, we decided what we'd do was to lock him in there. That'd teach him to have a lock on the outside!

Steam and acrid fumes of burnt bacon and guitar still belching out from the bathroom and the Frankie Vaughan record still repeating its ending over and over again, Batstooth and I put the plan into operation. With a screeching scrape that Eccles couldn't hear because of the noise of the roaring taps, I dragged a chair over to the toilet door. Then, in one fluid movement, I slammed the door and Batstooth leapt on the chair and drove the bolt home. Then, just for good measure, we wheeled the stereogram, castors squeaking, across to the toilet door and rammed it up against the door just to make sure he'd never get out. Frankie Vaughan's voice tremored a bit while this was going on but of course the stereogram had a floating turntable so that you could knock it and kick it around and the record would still play. The ending of 'Green Door' was still playing over and over. We turned the volume up. Blimey, it didn't half go loud. The sack stuff on the speakers buzzed and rattled; the windows shook. Eccles could be faintly heard shouting something. Then he started banging on the door. Something was upsetting him, OK. Whether it was the door being locked or the smoke and steam or the deafening 'Green Door, bomp-bomp!' playing over and over we didn't know, but we decided we might as well go home now and leave him to it.

Walking down the street, ten or twelve green doors along from Eccles's yellow door, we spotted Eccles's mother and Batstooth's mother turning the corner at the end of the street. You could still hear the record repeating over and over, partly because it was so loud and partly because we'd forgotten to shut the front door behind us. We were about to dive down an entry, but were too late. Batstooth's Ma had spotted us.

'Stanley!' she shouted. This was Batstooth's real name. We called him 'Batstooth' because he had teeth like a vampire bat and had to keep going to the dentist's to get them seen to.

Sheepishly, we crossed over to where they were waiting.

'I've been waiting for you!' said Mrs Batstooth. 'We've got to go to the dentist's.'

'Oh, what for?' moaned Batstooth.

'He wants to look up your arse to see if your hat's on straight. What do you think for?' she snapped, giving him a crack across the ear.

'I don't nay-go what's gay-getting' into this kid,' she said to Eccles's Ma, lapsing into scouse backslang.

Both mothers suddenly became aware of the noise coming from down the street. 'Green Door, . . .'

'Just listen to that racket,' said Mrs Eccles in disgust. 'Here am I, a 'ome-owner, 'avin' to put up wit' neighbours like that, makin' an almighty row.'

Batstooth and mother marching off to the dentist's, Mrs Eccles stormed off down the street to complain about the noise. But strangely enough, as she approached her yellow front door, the din seemed to get progressively louder.

This was a mystery to Mrs Eccles.

'Once he stepped forward to point something out'

2 Ale and Arty

'. . . and so, although there was no such thing as a Post-Impressionist School of painting from the point of view of style, in the sense that perhaps there may have been a distinct fusion of styles in other more unified Schools in Art History, that is in other more precisely defined areas, Van Gogh, Gauguin, Toulouse-Lautrec and Cézanne and, to a lesser extent, Signac and Seurat (who later, of course, formed the vanguard of the Pointillist movement) do tend, for convenience's sake, to be classified together as the Post-Impressionists . . .'

The plum-in-the-mouth voice droned on and on in the darkness; relief brought to the monotony of it all when this dithering, yawn-inducing twerp of a lecturer accidentally put a transparency of some timeless, boring work of art into the projector upside-down. By mistake, of course: he wouldn't have had the wit to do it on purpose, just for a laugh, to see whether any of his slumbering audience had noticed. He was wearing an immaculate, charcoal-grey suit, white shirt and a dark blue tie. His black, patent-leather hair was plastered down with Brylcreem. Brylcreem, in 1966! I ask you! And this guy's supposed to know something about art? He had huge ears, too. One of his ears stuck out like a Morris Minor indicator, the other was pressed close to his head, as if he'd spent thirty years or so with his head to the wall, listening to the noises made by the couple in the room next door to his lonely bed-sit. He just looked that kind of guy. Every now and then, as he moved about, bored restless by his own rhetoric, the light from the slide-projector burned redly through his sticking-out ear. Once he stepped forward to point something out and the bulging bum of a Rubens Venus flashed moment-arily across his back.

The bloke sitting next to me leaned over and hissed into my ear:

'Psst! Fancy a pint?'

Never able to say 'No', I concurred. It's often crossed my mind that, had I been born female, I'd have been a mother by the age of fifteen. At sixteen, I'd not yet entered a pub. Of course, I didn't admit as much to this bloke next to me. Keith, his name turned out to be. Tall, gangling, with shoulder-length hair, he'd been around a bit, you could tell, but I suspected he wasn't much older than I.

At long last, the lights went up for the tea-break interval. Blinking in the harsh fluorescent light, the motley collection of A-level Art evening-class candidates around us stretched, yawned and lit cigarettes. A sigh of relief went up all round. Earnest-looking middle-aged women wearing violently clash-ing tartan outfits, chiffon scarves and spectacles on chains scurried off down the bleak staircase of the Liverpool Institute High School, down into the bowels of that joyless building for a cup of tea and a chat.

Keith and I sloped off, ale-house bound.

'Fancy the Crack, or the Phil?' said Keith, breathing a deep sigh of satisfaction. Freedom at last. It was autumn and that special Liverpool 8 promise was in the air, crisp and fragrant. A small, perfectly round, golden moon beamed above shadowy Blackburne House, at that time a desirable Girls' High School.

The Phil,' I said promptly, never having set foot in either. I didn't know what or where the Phil was.

We walked a little farther on down Hope Street. Up ahead, the partially built, conical Roman Catholic Cathedral was fast disappearing in the misty, dark-blue evening. High above it, a huge but almost invisible crane bearing the legend TROLLOPE & COLLS in red neon was at rest, its day's work done. But the light had failed on & COLLS. So now there was this pure, matriarchal cathedral with the word TROLLOPE floating above it in supernaturally glowing letters. It seemed a deliberate heresy.

'It seemed a deliberate heresy'

Keith stopped abruptly outside a set of ornate, wrought-iron gates, set into an archway in the side of what looked like an elaborate Victorian gin-place, lights glowing like the *Titanic*. We stepped inside.

My carefully chosen rimless glasses promptly fogged up, as they were to do regularly over the next decade or so, upon entering the jam-packed bar of the Philharmonic Hotel. Wiping a spy-hole in the misty lenses, I saw an endless ebbing and flowing sea of Afghan coats, tinted spectacles and perky denim-clad bottoms, washing all around me. Long-haired men and longer-haired women stood talking and laughing against a backdrop of mahogany wood-panelling, brass, copper and stained-glass *fin-de-siècle* folly. High above me, some lettering in an exquisitely tinted window proclaimed: 'Music Is The Universal Language of Mankind.'

So this is what the inside of a pub looks like, I said to myself, as Keith, swaying this way and that, struggled back from the bar, complete with two foaming pints of bitter. Just behind him a man, whom I was sure I'd seen on the telly, seemed to be struggling to control the antics of a giant bird-eating spider. It turned out to be an Afghan hound which was thrusting its snout into passing crotches, causing squeals of surprise and a few sighs of disappointment. To the right was the sort of fireplace that characters from Henry James's novels would stand before, warming their tweed backsides while telling ghostly yarns, using freely words like 'singular' and 'tolerable'. A gaping mahogany and brass cavern, my view of it was largely obscured by the figure of a tall, bearded black man wearing a duffel-coat, apparently trying to sell strings of beads from a suitcase . . .

Struggling through the crowd, Keith and I eventually found a couple of vacant red-velvet armchairs in a huge hall that looked like a set from a Marx brothers film but which turned out to be the cocktail lounge. Over our heads, a vast and dangerous-looking crystal chandelier sparkled ostentatiously.

'Bet that thing would make your eyes water if it fell on your head, eh?' I chortled to Keith.

He ignored this remark. I was yet to learn that only tourists and weekend hippies were expected to comment on the décor at the Phil. It was considered uncool to do so, among the indigenous Liverpool 8 Bohemian circle. I had a lot to learn. Still, I was as yet only sixteen.

'That lecturer sure is a pain in the ass, man,' said Keith, in a contrived, mid-Atlantic accent.

'Sure is, man,' I burbled into my glass in a naturally un-glamorous, slightly urbanised scouse accent. In the sixties, all over Britain, it was the trendy thing to adopt a scouse accent. Everywhere except in Liverpool, of course. The sure way to turn off some slim, arty chick was to open your mouth and let a few flat scouse vowels drop out with a thud onto the marbled floor of the Phil.

'That bloke over there', muttered Keith *sotto voce*, 'is a famous poet. But don't look now.' He'd lapsed back into his own accent now, moving onto a different topic.

'In the sixties, all over Britain, it was the trendy thing to adopt a scouse accent'

A famous poet? I knew what 'famous' was and I knew what 'poet' was, but somehow the two didn't go together. I didn't realise that poets could be famous, though I fancied myself as one. But I'd been learning to play the guitar in order to get famous. Perhaps I needn't have bothered if, as Keith said, poets could get famous without learning to play the guitar. Ever the subtle one, I ignored Keith's 'Don't look now' and spun around in my chair, the better to view this phenomenon. I craned my neck in the direction of the famous poet, tilting my chair back onto two legs as I did so. Keith winced, pretending he wasn't with me. Unfortunately, these big armchairs have a point of balance which is not quite central, so, even though the angle my chair was at looked quite safe, in fact it wasn't. The chair began to tip over, quite slowly, but with a determined inevitability.

It's funny how time seems to stand still at certain points in

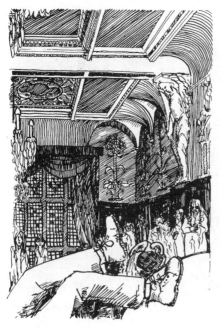

'It's funny how time seems to stand still at certain points in your life'

your life. This was one of them. As in a slow-motion film, the famous poet, wearing a fur coat, dark, ringletted hair and a wide-brimmed hat pulled down over his tinted granny-glasses, turned his head slowly and looked in my direction. I grinned foolishly back at him as the floor slowly but surely came up to meet me. Suddenly – crash! A kaleidoscope of flying pint glasses, shiny beaten-copper tabletops and a cascade of beer spun around my head as it made contact with the floor, inches away from the poet's pigskin boots.

It's funny also how at times like this you often say stupid things. I said a stupid thing on this occasion. Still grinning, I looked up from the floor, up into the famous nostrils of this poet, and said: 'Excuse me. I've never been here before.'

Then a marvellous thing happened. The poet said something which made me realise why he was a famous one. He said to me, quite quietly and sincerely, 'Oh, really? What do you think of the place?' – completely ignoring the fact that I was floundering about in broken glass and spilled beer. What a guy, I thought. I clambered to my feet, speechless and embarrassed, but indescribably thankful at the magnanimous way this man had handled the situation and my foolish antics. Still standing up to our knees in overturned tables and chairs, fragments of glass crunching underfoot, we struck up a conversation.

'Well, I like the place up to now,' I said, beaming at the scene of destruction all about me.

'It's not all it seems,' said the famous poet, offering me a cigarette. 'But what brings you here?'

I explained about the boring night-school lecture and was about to introduce Keith, when a glance in that direction showed Keith's chair, still standing, but now eloquently empty. He'd pissed off and left me, the twerp. I told the poet I was starting at the Art College up the road in a year or so, when I'd completed my foundation course. I also mentioned my poetry and guitar-playing.

'Oh, that's interesting,' he said. 'But you're wasting your time here in Liverpool. Edinburgh's the place to be. That's

31

where you'll get noticed. The Fringe is over for this year, but why don't you come up with us, me and my backing group, next year if you're still around? We can give you a lift.'

His words were still ringing in my ears a couple of pints later as I lurched out into the street. I wasn't used to all this beer. Even less was I used to the kind of stimulating conversation and sumptuous surroundings I'd found at the Phil. For the first time, but not the last, I was drunk, high as a kite. Drunk on beer, sure. But drunk also on life, on people, on me and my own future which then seemed to be sparkling up ahead of me, like a guiding star. I normally walk with a limp in one leg, but on that night I was limping with both legs, with my first bellyful of beer. It felt marvellous. I crossed Hardman Street, by the lights, stepping blithely in front of thundering great green buses, horns blaring angrily at this foolish youth staggering about among the traffic.

Proceeding erratically down the hill in the direction of the bus station, I passed a peculiar-looking building with a curved roof. O'Connor's Tavern, a sign proclaimed. Skidding to a halt outside, I glanced through the half-open green door. A torrid orange light bathed the interior in an enticing warm glow. From somewhere in the recesses of the building, I could hear a screaming electric guitar and a demented, jangling piano . . .

'There's an old piano and they play it hot behind the Green Door.'

The lines from a long-forgotten song entered my confused mind. A sinister-looking black bloke was lounging in the doorway.

'Hey, man,' he hissed. 'Wanna buy some draw?'

'Er, no. N-no, thanks,' I stammered, stepping back, a little frightened, but fascinated. I edged away slowly enough, hunching my shoulders as if expecting an attack from the rear, then accelerated and scurried off, zigzagging wildly down the street. Even in my confused state, I knew I must visit this place again. How come I'd lived in Liverpool all my life, yet this area, less than a mile from the familiar Ribble bus station, was all so new to me? It was a very different boy who fell into his quiet

'Liverpool College of Art and the Cathedral, Hope Street'

suburban bed that night, head spinning round and round: 'Green door, what's that secret you're keeping?'

So I was determined to find out what went on behind the green front door of O'Connor's Tavern. And it didn't take long. By now a first-year Fine Art student at Liverpool College of Art, I was soon caught up in the inevitable three-cornered social scene that went with this shrine of culture. The College of Art was *the* place to be at that time, the late 1960s, for Liverpudlians with leanings in the direction of art and the high life, not necessarily in that order. But, an impending merger with the Polytechnic being in the offing, the College was now becoming a difficult place to get into: I knew many young artists of exceptional abilities who couldn't get over the doorstep because they lacked the required O- and A-levels or for some other arbitrary reason known only to the College authorities. Although at that time, on looking back, I was a fairly mediocre artist and, indeed, a career as a commercial artist or a teacher seemed rather a dull prospect, I did have a handful of GCEs, so I was welcomed through the portals at my first attempt.

Yes, the College certainly had a high opinion of itself, in those days. Yet the only one of its sons who'd made a name for himself in any way at all was one John Lennon, who'd failed every examination in sight and had been kicked out of the place at an early stage.

However, during the period I attended the College, once you'd got over the initial hurdle of being offered a place on one of its courses, the rest was plain sailing. All you did was enjoy yourself, just doing the odd painting now and again to keep the authorities quiet. And, as I said, there was this fantastic three-cornered social scene. The three corners comprised the Phil, Ye Crack and O'Connor's Tavern. If ever you happened to be out alone at night, you knew that you could step into any one of these three hostelries and know immediately at least a dozen people in there. Liverpool 8, although only a mile from the city centre, was like a small enclosed village where everyone knew everyone else and few people strayed socially from a handful of regular drinking haunts. In fact, at that time, the height of the hippie era, it was downright dangerous to stray to another part of town where the local red-necks might take violent exception to people with long hair and sandals. Beatnik-beating was rapidly being superseded by hippie-bashing in the late sixties, although this seems bizarre today in a world where the staunchest pillars of society – bank-managers, teachers, policemen – can often be seen sporting longish hair and beards.

However, it was also in one's first year at Art College that an inevitable, though generally fairly brief, flirtation with drugs did blossom. And O'Connor's Tavern, I soon found out, was the place at which these commodities could be obtained. This was despite the fact that O'Connor's was situated right next door to the Liverpool Police Headquarters which occupied the corner of Hope Street and Hardman Street: the place must

34

'The Grapes, Egerton Street'

have been something of an embarrassment to the boys in blue.

Entering O'Connor's was a bit like stepping into a bar in Harlem. That profane orange glow gave the place a claustrophobic timelessness that was accentuated by the fact that, there being no windows, you could never be quite sure what time of day or night it was. Downstairs was a long bar running the full length of the single large room. A juke-box loudly pumped out the latest progressive rock and black music.

When empty, which wasn't often, the place used to remind me vividly of that desolate Van Gogh painting of a bar-room with red walls, a few slumped, down-and-out figures and a deserted pool-table. But mostly the place was full to capacity with jostling, strangely clad figures, the majority of whom were zonked out of their skulls on a variety of illegal substances. Upstairs, slightly more restrained avant-garde music and poetry evenings were held regularly, catering mainly for the student element.

Within seconds of your arrival on the scene, you were almost invariably accosted by a black guy asking if you wanted to score some dope. These blokes always seemed to rejoice in very prosaic English names such as Lawrence or Howard, despite their exotic appearance. If you were a bit green, as I was, you'd repair to the gents with one of these characters and with great cloak-and-dagger melodrama swap a couple of quid for a small silver-paper packet which, more often than not, contained nothing more mind-expanding than a few privet leaves or an artfully sliced piece of rubber brake-block from a bicycle. These con-men always got away scot-free, of course. You could hardly complain to the Consumers' Advice Council or quote the Trades Descriptions Act. Which is probably why, now I come to think of it, so many 'dope-pedlars' could operate with impunity only yards from the Police HQ. The simple fact was that many of them probably never handled anything that was genuinely illegal.

You soon got to know the genuine pushers, however. One such was a bearded black man by the name of Horace. On one occasion, a friend of mine, Bill Stevens, came down from Southport with ten quid, belonging to some mutual aquaint-ances, with which he'd been detailed to buy half an ounce of best-quality Lebanese hashish. Ten quid was not a sum to be sneezed at in those days. Bill located me one lunch-time in O'Connor's, although at that time I'd given up drinking alcohol, albeit temporarily, as I quickly discovered that some of the joys of teetotallism, such as insomnia and constipation, were experiences I could live without.

At this particular time, however, finding that a combination of dope-smoking and beer-drinking did nothing more cosmos-

*'Mike Hart, a singer of down'n'out
appearance but great ability,
performed regularly at
O'Connor's'*

'A poetry reading'

revealing for me than to make me violently sick, I'd taken instead to drinking pints of lime-juice. However this phase also was not to last long: I soon found out that anything more than a couple of glasses of lime-juice drunk during the course of an evening gave me violent pains in the guts, followed inevitably by embarrassing attacks of diarrhoea. Also, pint for pint, it was almost as expensive as beer, so this masochistic health-kick didn't even do my pocket any good. Eventually, I gave up both dope and lime-juice as a bad job and returned to trouble-free beer-drinking, which had the advantages that it was quite enlightening, very sociable, and you didn't have to pour it down the toilet in a state of panic every time a policeman looked as if he might be about to press the door-bell.

Through another acquaintance, a tall West Indian by the name of Johnny Barbados, I fixed up a rendezvous with Horace the pusher so that Bill Stevens could complete his lawless mission. This Johnny Barbados had himself, surprisingly enough, studied Law at University, though he had not completed the course. Apparently, he'd wanted to learn just enough about the law to be able to live outside of it with impunity.

Bill and I sat in a quiet corner of O'Connor's with Johnny to discuss business.

'First of all, go an' fetch t'ree beers,' he commanded, making as if to get some loose change out of his pocket. I went to the bar and came back with two pints of bitter and a glass of lime-juice. By this time, Johnny had forgotten about paying for the drinks. He quaffed half a pint in one gulp. Then he started muttering in a stage-whisper about Horace's dope, only raising his voice equally theatrically to proclaim: 'No, I haven't been to the pictures much lately!' when Jimmy Moore, the landlord, all ears, came bumbling past under the pretext of collecting empty glasses but casting suspicious glances in our direction.

The rendezvous fixed up, Bill and I decided to take a cobweb-clearing walk around the cathedral grounds until the time of our appointment with Horace – 2.30 p.m. outside

'Poets and musicians ("The Liverpool Scene") and friends outside O'Connor's, c. 1969'

O'Connor's. After an hour or so in the blazing sunshine, we strolled back to the now almost deserted bar.

No Horace. We should already have smelt a rat. But being a trifle naive, we didn't. We walked inside. There was Johnny, still sitting where we'd left him. We went over and sat next to him.

'Good afternoon, you ras-clats!' guffawed Johnny as if he hadn't seen us for years, slapping us violently on the shoulders. 'Were you been, boys? Go an' fetch t'ree beers!'

This time it was Bill who returned from the bar with two beers and a lime-juice. We edged the conversation back to the matter in hand.

'Horace? Oh, Horace I haven't seen for a while,' said Johnny. 'But I know where to find him. Just go and get t'ree mo' beers and I'll take you there.'

With an air of resignation, I made another trip to the bar and back. With all this lime-juice, strange burblings and churnings indicated that all was not as it should be in my abdominal parts. When Johnny was finally ready to leave, we stepped outside the gloomy bar once more into the blinding sunlight. Catching a bus outside – Bill paid the three fares – we alighted three stops later on Princes Avenue. Crossing the boulevard, Johnny took us into a place called the Federal Club. I paid the three admission fees.

When our eyes had become accustomed once more to the gloom, Bill and I realised we were the only whites in the place. All around, under the eerie glow of the muted ultra-violet lights, were rows of electric-lilac teeth and rolling eyes. Little was discernible and we began feeling decidedly uncomfortable.

'Tell you what . . .' began Johnny.

'Don't tell me: go and get three beers.' Bill finished the sentence off for him, groping his way to the bar. Meanwhile, Krakatoa-like explosions erupting in my nether regions, I had more urgent business elsewhere and blundered off to find the gents.

Upon my return, a sinister-looking guy with shaven skull and sharp mohair suit was muttering earnestly to Johnny. I wouldn't be at all surprised if this conversation concerned our ten quid I mused, at last beginning to consider that perhaps things weren't going quite according to plan. Having apparently reached a satisfactory conclusion to their discussion, Johnny and the Skull were about to tell us something, probably to our disadvantage, when, like the Cavalry coming over the hill, up stepped a beaming Horace. Boy, were we glad to see him. Although he too was of unprepossessing appearance, compared to this black Yul Brynner he looked positively angelic.

'Hi, there, Spar!' said Horace to me, grinning broadly. However – perhaps it was my imagination playing tricks – I could have sworn I saw him give a sly wink to Johnny and his shiny-pated crony. When we'd hurriedly explained the nature of our business, Horace said: 'No problem. Come with me.'

'Discussing something, probably to our disadvantage'

'Sure you wouldn't like a beer before we go?' I said drily. But sarcasm was wasted on Horace.

'No, I don't drink, lah. The kind of stuff I got for you, you won't need no drink. Blow your head off, lah.'

Back yet again out in the sunshine, we walked a couple of hundred yards onto the main drag. Upper Parliament Street. I'd heard of this ghetto area before, but had not yet been there. Swarms of spidery-limbed, brown-skinned children were running everywhere, their ample mommas sitting on the steps of the towering, dilapidated old houses, chatting idly in the sun. At one particular building, covered in flaking pink paint that looked like human skin after a bad case of sunburn, Horace stopped and said, 'You two wait here. Ten quid deal, you say?'

Bill produced ten crumpled pound notes. Horace snatched them off him, rather hurriedly I thought, and loped up the steps and into the recesses of the shabby-looking dwelling.

Five minutes passed by. 'Hope this guy hurries up. I'll be needing a crap again soon,' I muttered, agitated. Bill got out his ciggies.

'Here, have a smoke. Take your mind off it. I always have a ciggie when I'm waiting for someone. When you've smoked one, you know seven minutes or so is up.'

Two cigarettes each later, there was still no sign of Horace.

'D'you think something's up?' queried Bill.

'No, he's probably got it hidden somewhere. You can't be too careful you know,' I said in man-of-the-world tones, but wishing I felt as confident as I fondly imagined I sounded.

Another ten minutes on, Bill at last said: 'Right. That's it. I'm going to see what's happening.' He stepped up to the front door and rang the bell stridently. In due course a haggard but friendly-looking white woman, probably in her early thirties but looking forty, came to the door.

'Sorry to bother you, love, but have you seen a bloke named Horace?'

'Horace? Oh, yeah. He came in about half an hour ago.'

'Can we speak to him?'

'Well, no. He came in but he went straight out the back door. I think he said he was going to some place to play cards.'

'Oh, my God, oh no,' groaned Bill as we walked slowly away. 'What am I going to tell the lads?'

He flopped down on the memorial bench outside the nurses' home on the corner of Parliament Street and Princes Avenue, head held in his hands.

Me? I preferred to stand. Something unpleasant had just happened in my trousers.

' "Roll over, Beardsley" — scene from a Pseudo-Regency nightclub'

3   *The Road to the Lucky Bar*

'. . . 'Ere. Give us a lift with this, pal.'

I'd been sitting dolefully staring into space, half watching this bloke fiddling about with his disco equipment and half day-dreaming.

'OK,' I said. I propped my sketch-pad against the wall, hauled myself out of my seat, and helped him to lift a large speaker-cabinet onto a table.

'Ta . . . you're the artist, aren't you?'

'I suppose you could call me that,' I mumbled as I draped myself back across my chair. If you could call these dull, pretentious portraits I produced in this dull, pretentious discothèque 'art'.

'Let's have a look at some of your work,' he persisted.

I showed him some of my sample drawings. I called them 'samples', but they were really just rejects. Jokers who'd had me sketch their portraits, just for a laugh, but who'd had no intention of paying me the modest fee I was asking and handed them back to me with a derisory 'Don't look nothing like me.' On some bad nights, I seemed to get one time-wasting idiot after another like this and went home penniless in the small hours, wondering how I was going to break the bad news to my patiently waiting wife. Three kids slumbering upstairs and not even a slice of stale bread in the house, eating cauliflower-cheese every night because by the time all the bills had been paid there was nothing left over for luxuries like food. I often reflected bitterly on this 'romantic' artist's life I was leading, now in my late twenties and worse off than ever before. My mind-bendingly boring day-time job in a department store was paying ten pounds a week less than what the dole had to offer. Was I going crazy, or what? Ten years previously, the world had seemed to be waiting at my feet. Handing the DJ my sketch-pad to look at, I glanced across at the mirror at the back of the bar. Staring back at me was a wild-looking figure with shoulder-length straggling hair. Gaunt, hollow cheekbones forced their way through a sparse, untidy beard. Haunted, desperate eyes could be discerned behind a pair of dark glasses with a crack right across one lens and a sticking plaster anchoring the ear-piece to the frame. The figure was dressed in ill-fitting, second-hand clothes. He looked like a man who'd given up.

Meanwhile, the strapping, sun-tanned, healthy-looking DJ was flicking through my 'samples'.

'You know, you're wasting your time in here, mate. The divvies who come in here wouldn't appreciate this sort of thing. You know where you wanna go? A placed called the Lucky Bar.'

The Lucky Bar?

'Never heard of it,' I said. Neither was I interested in moving on to yet another soulless, lifeless, artificial discothèque. Despite this, through force of habit, I asked him where it was.

'Meanwhile, the DJ was flicking through my "samples" '

'Parliament Street. Down the bottom end, by the docks. All the sailors go in there, looking for hoo-ahs.'

Parliament Street? Jesus. I've not reached those depths yet. Not *yet*, anyway. No way am I going to trot around Parliament Street all night.

'I tell you, you'll never look back. Just knock on the door and say Billy sent you. You can't miss it – it's got a green door.'

A green door.

'Just give it a try. You've got nothing to lose. It's open all

49

night, so you could still work here till two o'clock and then move on up there. But I'll tell you for nothing, you're wasting your time here, boy.'

'You bloody fool!'

I shouted, almost in tears through anger and frustration. A lad of about sixteen, obviously the worse for drink, had just barged into me as I stepped off a 72 bus at the bottom of Hardman Street one night on my way to work.

'Sorry, mate,' the lad mumbled, beating a hasty retreat.

Now what am I going to do, I moaned to myself. Under one arm was my sketch-pad, under the other was a large, flat parcel wrapped in newspaper. It crunched and tinkled ominously. Oh no, oh no, oh no. A few weeks previously, in a desperate attempt to raise some cash in order to placate my bank-manager and pay a few bills, I'd winkled out an advance payment from the manager of the club I was then working at on a series of stained-glass windows I'd agreed to design and make for the bar-room. Tonight, well behind schedule, I was delivering them; 'was' now being the operative word.

I stormed off down among the labyrinth of streets which comprised Disco Land. Arriving at my destination, I prodded the door-bell loud and long with an impatient forefinger. If one of those blasted doormen in their monkey-suits says just one word to me about not wearing a tie again – just one word – I resolved venomously, I'd smash the remains of these windows over his head, even though he'd probably beat me to a pulp.

The door opened. I barged through and headed straight for the manager's office. Walking in, I said 'Here's your windows, Harry!' and dropped the parcel with a crash, flat onto his desk.

'What's the matter with you, pal? Gone round the bloody bend?' gasped a startled Harry, his dickey-bow almost spinning round in amazement.

I calmed down enough to explain what had happened. He wasn't a bad sort, Harry. Although the manager, he was really just a dog's body to the owners of the club, flash, womanising playboy types who came in dressed like millionaires and posed about the place all night, attractive but brainless young women on each arm. Meanwhile, Harry could often be found sluicing out the gents or sacking a barmaid, caught with her hand in the till. All the unpleasant jobs were left to Harry.

'Oh, don't worry about it, son,' he said reassuringly. 'Just do 'em again in your own time. There's no rush; in the meantime, here's a couple of quid to keep you going.'

'God bless you, Harry,' I said, and left the office.

I strolled around the already-busy club, surveying the scene. A large, pseudo-Regency place, everything about it was phoney. Even the authentic-looking wattle and daub and oaken beams were chunks of plaster, painted dark-brown and off-white. God, I hate this place, I thought. These clubs are fine if, like the majority of the punters, you arrive already half-pissed and complete the process during the next couple of hours. But if, like me, you were trying to abstract a living from the place, staying stone-cold sober, you really saw humanity at its crummiest. Glossy young couples looking as if they'd just stepped out of a fashion-store window would completely shatter the illusion of elegance as soon as they opened their mouths. Alongside the customers, the surroundings seemed to improve slightly. But not much. Even the computerised disco music in the place was no more than musical wallpaper – an anaesthetic to ensure that if the beer and the appalling décor didn't numb your brain, the music would.

While waiting for my first customer, I stood scowling at the DJ stand. One of the owners of the place had decided to try his hand at being a DJ and was cavorting about on the dais, a gleaming grin on his face, extolling the virtues of the club:

'Chicken-in-the-basket, one pound fifty,' he babbled.

'Daylight robbery,' I shouted back, adopting momentarily a grin as vacuous as his own, giving him the thumbs-up sign, then lapsing back into my natural scowl. He waved gaily back at me, unable of course to hear what I was saying.

'Three luxurious bars . . .!' he went on, burbling into the microphone with transparent insincerity.

'None of which you can get served at and all selling over-priced, highly toxic, watered-down badger-piss!' I bellowed back at him, with a grin that was giving me ear-ache. He nodded and smiled, returning my waves and exaggerated thumbs-up signs.

Quickly tiring of this game, however, I noticed the regular DJ standing behind me. He, too, was scowling. He stood with his Benidorm-tanned arms folded and wore a green tee-shirt with the words 'Toothickfor University' printed across it. His spindly legs were encased in cripplingly tight jeans festooned with zips in all the wrong places, such as across the knee. However, he wasn't as bad as he looked, this bloke, and we often used to swap complaints about the punters and the management.

'Just look at that posin' bastard,' he muttered, as the other would-be DJ attempted to place a record on the turntable amid much over-amplified hissing and scratching. He couldn't seem to locate the beginning of the record with the pick-up arm on the disco equipment.

'I'm looking,' I said. The joke now wearing off, my stony face must have been reminiscent of Winston Churchill with toothache.

'Anyway,' the DJ continued, 'what are you doing, still here? I told you the place to go. The Lucky Bar. Just tell 'em Billy sent you. You don't have to hang around this dump.'

Deciding that the punters were probably by now pissed enough to have their portraits done, I wandered off around the room, sketch-pad at the ready.

Despite their extrovert, loud-mouthed behaviour, a good many scousers are quite self-conscious and although vanity often made them stop me and ask for a portrait, they seemed to have great difficulty in just sitting still for ten minutes. While I was struggling to produce a recognisable likeness, the sitter would be shifting and dodging about in his seat, winking and waving to his mates, pulling faces, straightening or ruffling his hair, lighting cigarettes, scratching his balls, any god-damn thing except just sitting still. And, on this particular night, I got

52

'Portrait of the artist, tearing his hair out over difficult customers'

a few of these jokers, one after another. Just what I needed.

Suddenly, one of the doormen, looking like a bloated King Penguin in his dinner-suit, white shirt and dickey-bow, approached stiffly and said to me:

'There's a mate of yours at the door.'

I obediently walked to the door, the King Penguin following me the way those at the zoo follow the keeper around with his bucket of fish.

There, standing in the doorway, was an old friend of mine, Barney Neildun. A second engineer in the Merchant Navy, he usually looked me up whenever he was ashore.

'Hello, Barney,' I said, glad to see a human face. 'Come in and have a drink.'

But just then the King Penguin stepped forward.

'Oh no you don't, pal,' he said gruffly, barring the doorway with an arm like a tree-trunk. 'Not with those boots, you don't. And you haven't got a tie on. And you're not a member. There's nothing down for you, pal.' Bouncers always call you 'pal' when they're at their most obtuse.

I looked down at Barney's feet. He had on a magnificent pair of Spanish-leather thigh-boots. Probably worth a hundred quid or more. Under his lumberjack coat he was wearing a thick seaman's jersey and a pair of cords. All good, sound, sensible clobber. I looked around at the ordinary punters walking unimpeded into the club, with their ten-quid imitation-leather shoes, tissue-thin suits with no lining and jackets that looked as if the wearer had forgotten to remove the coat-hanger before donning them.

'Right. That does it. Come on, Barney. Let's get out of this bloody place.'

I ducked under the King Penguin's mighty arm and joined Barney in the street. A taxi happened to be passing and we jumped in.

'Take us to the Lucky Bar, please. Upper Parliament Street.'

The taxi cruised slowly down Parliament Street. All around, in what had once been that grimy but vital ghetto, buildings had been demolished to make way for new barrack-like blocks of flats and plantations of already-vandalised young trees. The myriad of late-drinking clubs had dwindled down to a mere half-dozen or so. On the right-hand side, we passed the only Parliament Street club I'd as yet felt was safe enough to enter – the Somali. We passed also the gargantuan, spooky outline of the Anglican cathedral.

'What did you say this place was called?' said the cabbie, peering left and right.

'The Lucky Bar', I said. 'Should be just about here. We'll get out anyway. Keep the change.' The cabbie blinked at the pound note I'd given him, then blinked at his meter which read £1.05.

Barney and I found ourselves standing outside an innocuous-looking, double-fronted Victorian house, on the usual rambling Liverpool 8 scale. The brickwork, we could see by the light of a street-lamp, was painted a deep red colour. A small illuminated sign proclaiming WINE, DINE AND DANCE AT THE ALL NATIONS CLUB was situated above the front door. The name meant nothing: most Toxteth dives have both an official name and a popular name. The important thing was the colour of the front door – green. This was the night I was going to find out, once and for all, what did go on behind the Green Door.

For some reason, I was hesitant now. It took Barney, usually the timid one in our occasional partnership, to step up and ring the bell. The door opened promptly to reveal, not another King Penguin, not a burly, surly, black man, but a very average-looking young lad of about eighteen in grimy tee-shirt, faded blue jeans and white plimsolls.

'Yeah?' he said nonchalantly, his jaws grinding on a piece of chewing gum. ('When I said Joe sent me, someone laughed out loud behind the Green Door!')

'Er . . . can I speak to the boss,' I said, slightly taken aback. I had rather been expecting the usual type of aggressive slob that clubs employ, downtown, to filter the would-be clientele queuing at the portals.

'Yeah.'

Using the same monosyllable but with a slight variation of tone, he turned back into the club, his slight frame silhouetted in an orange glow that caused a few forgotten rusty bells to chime a cracked melody in my mind. Shortly a small, also slightly built, ginger-bearded bloke with thinning blond hair took his place at the door. He was wearing an open-necked shirt and corduroy trousers.

'Yeah?'

'Well, I wanted to see the boss, really.'

'I am the boss. It's me Dad's club, but I run it.'

For some reason, I'd still been expecting to see a flamboyant playboy, the kind of boss I was used to. Exasperated with my aimless dithering, Barney now stepped in:

'My friend here is an artist. Draws portraits. I'm his agent. We'd like to know if we can come into your club to work. We've worked in some of the best night-spots in Europe . . .'

Before Barney got too carried away and started reeling off a list of the crowned heads of Western civilisation who'd been privileged enough to sit for me, I decided I'd better interrupt.

'Is it OK if we come in, then?'

'Well, it's OK by me. As long as you don't mind having the odd pint spilled over your head. Get some funny customers in here sometimes.'

This was the first time I'd heard a club-owner admit that his patrons were anything less than the *crème de la crème* of sophisticated night-people.

'Well, that's a chance we'll have to take,' I breezed airily. Next second we were inside.

First impressions are funny things. Like my wife often says, when you see a newborn baby's face for the first time, you see the man he's going to be. Just for a flashing moment. Then he reverts to being a bug-eyed, chubby-cheeked, bouncing babe. It was a bit like that with the Lucky. I saw, in my first glance around that small bar-room, the shape of my life for the next couple of years, at least.

It was a scruffy place: it was dirty, seedy. It smelt a bit, too. But it had an instant, exciting atmosphere like nowhere else. Small, it was just a parlour, the windows screened off so that no lights could be seen from the street. There were ships' lifebelts on the walls, Salvador Dali reproductions, bullfight posters, African masks, obscene postcards and dozens of quirky, blurred flashlight snapshots of drunken revellers. All the sort of things you'd expect to see in a sailor's cabin, in fact. Along the back wall, directly opposite the blanked-out windows, was the bar, decked out with a bizarre, kitsch, selection of knick-knacks. On a shelf behind the bar was a tank of variously coloured fantail goldfish, drifting gracefully and timelessly about. From the centre of the ceiling hung a glittering, many-faceted silver sphere, the type that used to be common in provincial ballrooms. It turned slowly from left to right on its own axis.

The next thing I noticed was the music. Instead of the usual expensive and deafening array of disco equipment, there was simply a juke-box, over there in a corner by the bar. I remember the record that happened to be playing was 'The Spider and the Fly' by the Rolling Stones, a cheeky, slinky blues number

'Lucky Bar people'

which I'd not heard for at least ten years or so. I was soon to find that the juke-box selection was rich in this rhythm-and-blues music from the sixties which made such a welcome change from all of that disco pap and endless BeeGees records, all sounding as if they were conceived by means of a test-tube. There were some contemporary records amongst the oldies, but good ones, chosen by someone who knew what he was doing: stuff like The Pretenders, Sex Pistols, The Police, Blondie, Stevie Wonder. Stuff that made you feel the blood run in your veins, stuff that made you feel good. Instead of stuff that made you feel like you were wandering around a supermarket.

And then, of course, there were the people.

Barney and I were standing in what had once been the hallway of this house, and we looked in on the bar-room from a doorway leading off the passage. Barney said he'd seen places like this before. In Bangkok, Hamburg, New Orleans. For the first time in years, in fact for the first time since that night I'd hovered, a drunken teenager, at the doorway of O'Connor's Tavern, I felt that something was going on here, something I'd not yet experienced, but something I'd like to have been a part of. 'All I want to do is join the happy crowd behind the Green Door!'

The place had a wild, party atmosphere. Party? No, the word is too mild: Mardi Gras would be better. The women, glossy and exotic, varied from ageing madames to bright-eyed girls in their late teens. The thing that struck me was the sheer individuality of these women. Some looked dressed for a sumptuous, ritzy dinner-party in some remote millionaire's chateau, others wore simple jeans and tee-shirts. As they danced in the middle of the floor, you could sense that they were feeling the music from head to toe, improvising their funky little dance routines as they went along. A complete contrast to that appalling disco crowd, where the blokes would hop about in their flared trousers like mindless marionettes while their blank-faced, gum-chewing girlfriends stared into space, shifting almost imperceptibly from one foot to another.

The men at the Lucky, I soon realised, were nearly all foreign seamen of various nationalities and colours. During the course of the next couple of years I was to come into contact here with Norwegians, Danes, Swedes, Russians, Icelanders, Portuguese, Spaniards, Turks, Libyans, Americans, Canadians, Chileans, Argentinians, Malaysians, Japanese and Chinese. Oh, and one Welshman, Taffy. He turned up regularly, several times a week, taking a taxi up from Wales each night and back the following morning, fifty quid lighter. He'd come into some hefty redundancy pay when his local steelworks had closed down and, the hillsides of his homeland not offering quite the kind of welcome he sought, he took to commuting back and forth to Liverpool in this extravagant manner. But mostly the blokes here were tough but generous seamen, out to have a good time, temporarily released from their floating prisons. And there was no way the management could have insisted on *this* lot wearing ties, even if it had wanted to, which it didn't. Individuality was definitely the order of the day. Some blokes chose to wear the traditional sailor outfits, others wore their engine-room clobber; still others wore casual but expensive gear – leather, suede and so on – picked up from remote corners of the globe.

The international atmosphere was all-pervasive: even the gents, atop a flight of stairs, was marked HERREN. Barney and I sat at the foot of these steps on this, my first night at the Lucky, and fell into contemplation. Across the passage was another small room where a few couples sat quietly talking and drinking. People were drifting to and fro across the passage, laughing, glass in hand, and speaking either broken English or scouse backslang. I noticed that the women seemed to speak to their beaux for the evening in the same accents that the foreigners used, possibly to make them feel at home but more likely because most scousers are natural mimics. I got out some pencils to sharpen with a pocket-knife. A waitress was passing.

'Got an ashtray, love?' I asked, looking around for somewhere to deposit the pencil shavings.

'Oh, just drop 'em on the floor, babe. They'll get swept up. Fellows who come in here, they spend over a hundred quid a night. They're not bothered about the way the place looks. They get what they want here.'

Again, a sharp contrast in attitudes to that which I had been used to. It began to dawn on me that indeed there was a lot of money about in this place. A tall, handsome Irish lady approached me. Attached to her arm was a refined-looking gentleman with silver hair and gold-rimmed spectacles. He wore an immaculately tailored suit and, apparently, spoke no English.

'Dis chentleman's da Captain of da *Atlahntic Queen*. He'd loik ter know ho' mutch yer chorge fer yer drorr'n's,' the lady said with a rich brogue. Making an instinctive, snap decision, I doubled my usual price. I waited for a reaction as she conferred with the captain.

She turned back to me: 'He says dat's very cheap, now. He paid ten toimes dat in Morocco and it wasn't half as gude as yours. He wants yer ter dror me an' den hum.'

I sketched them both, the man shook my hand warmly and gave me a generous tip.

'This place is going to be OK, Barney,' said I.

'The Somali'

4 On the Game

During the Lucky Bar period, my working day would begin at around eleven o'clock p.m. I'd pick up my sketch-pad and graphite sticks, kiss my wife cheerio and walk the mile or so to work, down Princes Avenue. Upper Parliament Street is the main artery running through the crumbling, cosmopolitan village and often my first port of call was here at a combined restaurant and drinking-club frequented chiefly by Somalis.

The doorman here was an incredible character, a giant of a man who apparently had never had a real name given him. Legend had it that his former occupation had been government hangman, back in his native land. Everyone in the club called him simply – and wisely – 'Boss'. As favoured drinking haunts ebb and flow in popularity, the bona-fide clientele at the Somali was sometimes in danger of being elbowed out by an influx of students and trendies – middle-class boozers bent on seeing how the other half lived – but if you'd dared to point this out, of course, you'd be accused of inverted snobbery.

Not all of the whites in here were tourists, however – not by a long chalk. Take Dot, for instance, a 'magic mushroom' fanatic. She laughed in the faces of the Drugs Squad, stoned out of her lid on powerful but legal fungi, picked in Sefton Park. With her long red hair and even redder wellington boots, she could often be seen gyrating about the place, doing her own dance, 'The Carlsberg Shuffle', aided by a potent brew bearing that name whenever mushrooms were out of season.

Neither, of course, was Lily a tourist. Nor was her smiling half-caste son Brian, whose ambition it was to be an artist. And still is, though these days he works for a local newspaper. Lily works behind the bar with her sister Sally, a formidable Irish lady, who ran the place with her rotund and jolly Somali husband, the redoubtable Mr Mahmoud.

I used to stop here, ostensibly to get my supply of cigarettes for the night. But if the place wasn't too packed, I'd enjoy a quiet beer – my first of the day and, if it was to be a busy night, quite often my last. This drink plus a bag of peanuts would set me up for the night, in readiness for the bedlam I was likely to be stepping into farther on into the small hours.

From here, I'd proceed a hundred yards or so, in the shadow of the Anglican Cathedral, down the hill towards the docks. Stopping at a basement light in one of the large terraced townhouses that flanked the street, I'd descend the short flight of steps into the steamy cellar club which jumps and throbs seven nights a week. This is the Alahram, of which more in a later chapter. The beefy half-caste doorman would greet me with a gleaming smile. After exchanging pleasantries with him, I'd start work. The air here – what there was of it – was dense with loud Jamaican reggae, interspersed with the better commercial disco sounds and the odd Yemeni folk recording. The punters consisted mainly of Arabs, Iranians and Libyans, plus a smattering of scouse drunkards who occasionally wandered in.

On a good night, moving from table to table with my sketch-pad I'd go through the place like the proverbial dose of salts. But on a bad night, I might have been standing around doing nothing for protracted periods, awaiting a customer. When I'd exhausted the night's supply of punters wanting their portraits done, I'd leave the club and cross the street to the Lucky Bar.

Newcomers at the Lucky often had difficulty in accepting that the girls in there, many of whom were very attractive and sophisticated in appearance, were – almost without exception – prostitutes. Once I'd become part of the furniture there, the girls seemed to accept my presence in a sisterly sort of way – realising probably that my game differed only technically from

'Waiting for business at the Lucky'

their own. I was never mistaken for a potential client: standing among them at the bar they'd inquire chattily after the health of my wife and kids as we'd all hang about waiting for customers. Also I was often the only male in the place who could speak English, apart from the itinerant crew of taxi-drivers, photographers and plain-clothes CID men, all of whom, in their various ways, were making a living in this nocturnal society.

Usually as the first light of dawn cast an eerie blue-gold light upon the church opposite, I'd emerge at last from the still-bouncing clip-joint and flop into one of the several taxis waiting outside like great shiny black carrion beetles waiting for the richer pickings – philanthropic seamen – still to come. The drivers nearly all knew me by now and one of them would whisk me away on my brief journey home, often foregoing a handsome tip from a foreign sailor to do so.

The Lucky Bar was open all night, every night. Depending upon which ships were in dock, it could just as easily be chock-full on, say, a Tuesday night as on a Saturday. The 'business-girls', as they called themselves, advised me to do as they did when trying to predict whether the club would be financially worth a visit or not: get hold of a copy of *Lloyd's List* or some similar paper which gave details of which ships were due in to the Port of Liverpool. Ships could, of course, dock at any time of day or night. Frequently, the Lucky would be almost entirely devoid of male company, the girls sitting quietly around the place, waiting. But at any time the doorbell might ring and in would pour a gang of freshly docked 'mushers' (seamen) ready for anything, wallets bulging, banknotes flying like confetti.

This place, I knew, was one of the last strongholds of old Liverpool – Maggie May's stomping ground: a big international port, the biggest in the world, nine miles of docks, the gateway to the Americas. Now a pathetic shadow of its former self, the mighty port seemed to be suffering its death-throes. Even the prostitutes – who, incidentally, flitted around the ports of Europe, stowed away in some cabin, with almost as

'Maggie, Maggie May, they have taken her away'

much nonchalance and regularity as did their men – knew that Rotterdam was now the place to be in, all major shipping trade having moved eastward and southward as a result of Britain's EEC membership.

The Lucky Bar, too, was dying on its feet: a demolition order had already been served when I discovered the place – a casualty of the local authority's latest white elephant, the famous Inner City Ring Road. Today, there's not even a trace of it, not even so much as a hole in the ground. Or a plaque. Yet it had been, in its heyday, virtually a living, breathing museum of an aspect of Liverpool's social history which can never be repeated, to the hypocritical relief of a few but to the great regret of many. A victim, in fact, of the same kind of mentality which ordered the demolition of the Cavern Club, made famous by the Beatles in the 1960s, leaving American tourists to come thousands of miles to gawp at a piece of derelict waste-ground.

'The Cavern Club, which went the same way as the Lucky Bar'

The Lucky Bar and other establishments which occupy the so-called 'twilight zones' were, like everywhere else, hit by financial recession. The poverty in Liverpool is notorious: even foreign seamen were aware of it. I remember the place being referred to by them as a 'chocolate port'. This was a name they gave to any run-down port where they knew they could step ashore and get their 'fucky-fuck' for a fraction of the going rate if they played their cards right.

All 'business-girls' are, of course, great survivors. They've all moved on to pastures new: yet they can find nowhere with the magic of the Lucky. There seems to be nowhere quite like it. Where else, for example, amid all of that nightly wheeling and dealing, could you hold a conversation with an attractive woman of Arab stock who'd discuss, in a scouse accent so thick you could spread it on a butty, the latest draft of a book she'd been writing on Boris Pasternak?

Where else could you find cranium-cracking cocktails with names like Red Witch or Manhattan Special, selling for a couple of quid a glass?

'Business-girls, homeward-bound after a hard day's night'

And finally, where else could those crazy incidents occur that were commonplace at the Lucky?

Take, for example, the night a very odd couple approached me. Stern-looking, very sober, I thought at first that they were police. But the woman produced from her bag a sketch I'd apparently done of her a few weeks previously, though I didn't recall it.

'This is your work, isn't it?' she asked.

Oh, here we go, I said to myself. Wants her money back because the sketch doesn't make her look sufficiently like Racquel Welch.

'Yeah,' I said, after giving the drawing a lengthy scrutiny, in order to create the impression it just *might* have been perpetrated by someone else.

'Thought so. I've been all round the clubs looking for you. Couldn't remember where I'd had this picture done. But you live locally, don't you? Married, three kids. Had some trouble with your leg as a child . . .'

She went on like this for a while, as if mentally ticking off items in a notebook. Though I had nothing to conceal, I was annoyed: in a way, it gave me the cold shudders to think that in a supposedly free country a complete stranger could have details of my personal life at her fingertips. There was something a bit sinister about this.

The police I'd already ruled out: when out on the town, they generally prefer to live and let live, though a copper did once ask me if I fancied doing identikit sketches if ever the occasion arose. This offer I'd obviously turned down: most of my customers lived and worked slightly on the wrong side of the law and if word got around that I'd even thought about working for 'the busies', I'd have run the risk of losing a lot of hard-earned trust, not to mention a good chance of getting my head kicked in. In any case, this odd couple looked far too intense to be coppers. Although the man remained studiously silent throughout, eventually the woman ceased her interrogation of me to at last broach the subject she'd been building up towards.

Apparently, she was a journalist. The paper she worked for sent her regularly out to the Middle East to cover dodgy subjects like public floggings and worse. The problem was, these operations were so hush-hush that they didn't dare send a photographer to accompany her. After putting their heads together, her employers had decided that what was required was an artist. Preferably someone used to working quickly and accurately under less than ideal conditions. This, apparently, was where I came in.

I had a momentary vision of myself standing in some sun-baked foreign courtyard, surreptitiously sketching someone having his head chopped off. But she quickly allayed these fears before they were voiced by telling me that all the artist had to do was to observe whatever was going on, making a few mental notes, then return to the luxury accommodation that went with the job and do a few sketches. For a phenomenal fee, I might add.

All of this sounded so utterly far-fetched that I thought it might just about be genuine. However, I wasn't about to seriously consider it. For a start, I didn't see it all fitting in too well with my family commitments. In any case, life here in Liverpool was quite sufficiently hair-raising, thanks. Besides, I felt that at last I'd carved a little niche for myself on my own home patch; by my own erratic standards, I'd settled down to a steady workaday (well, workanight) routine.

All the same, my own journalistic instincts made me want to draw out some more information. How, for example, had *she* got into this curious business?

The story she gave me was that, upon the sudden and tragic death of her young husband, she had become so distraught that doctors, noting that she was a writer, urged her to use the event as a kind of catharsis; to write down in painful but crystal-clear detail the events leading up to her husband's death and to describe her own emotions with equal clarity. It seemed that her Editor, on seeing this, was so impressed with her hitherto unsuspected gifts for probing a situation, had quickly promoted her to a 'star' position and begun sending her out on these exotic missions.

I told the couple the various reasons why I would decline their offer. They readily saw my point and said that in any case their search for a likely candidate was still at an early stage, although my credentials seemed sound enough. In fact, up until this point, they'd only come upon one other person working in a similar field to mine but had had to eliminate him as a possible candidate because he'd had a number of criminal convictions. The prospect of working alongside a criminal *per se* didn't bother them: it was just that his record would cause endless visa, passport and work-permit problems while travelling abroad.

Although I never saw this woman again, I did meet the man by chance once. Upon my asking what became of their search for an artist, he told me they'd eventually tracked down a gifted eighteen-year-old art student who was a part-time ornithologist and who, in his spare time, trudged through marshes sketching wild birds on the wing. He'd jumped at the chance of taking up this unusual post and negotiations were under way.

The Lucky Bar – strange that a place like this should have a vernacular name that made it sound like a bar of chocolate – wasn't all high drama, of course. Many lighter moments cropped up.

One such was the occasion I accidentally locked myself in the toilet – served me right for doing it to Eccles, all those years ago. The novely of having unlimited time to read all the graffiti – 'Paint it again, Sam', 'I Stink, Therefore I Am', 'Dyslexia Rules, KO' – soon wore off and I began hammering and banging. As luck would have it, nobody else had the urge to use the HERREN at that time and I was in there for almost ten minutes before being rescued by a man wearing a pair of pyjamas and carrying a copy of *Vanity Fayre* under his arm. Though I'm not easily surprised, I must admit I had to do a double-take on this bloke, grateful though I was for his timely appearance. His tousled hair was standing on end; his bleary eyes and rumpled mien gave every impression of a man who'd just been called reluctantly from his bed.

Which, it turned out, is exactly what he was. I found out that his name was Arthur and he was one of the two tenants who occupied a pair of grim bed-sitters on the second floor of the building. Falling into conversation, I found he was an interesting and very well-read bloke who suffered from a drink-problem which, of course, was aggravated not a little by the fact that he lived above one of the wildest clip-joints in town. He enjoyed almost twenty-four-hour access to the bar, the owners allowing him the odd nip or two during the quiescent daylight hours in return for his services as a kind of caretaker.

The other tenant was Komo, a white-haired black man in his seventies. He could often be seen in a side-room on cold winter nights, sitting gazing into the gas-fire, slowly rubbing his hands, oblivious to all around him. I've often wondered what became of Arthur and Komo after the demolition of the Lucky.

It's easy to imagine many fortunes being made and lost at the Lucky Bar at various points in its history. I only caught the tail-end of it. I suppose to many the place was just an irksome embarrassment. To me, it represented a very special part of the life and times of a very special city.

It was the last Green Door to be opened up to me: now it's closed forever.

'The Shadow, doing his stuff on Parliament Street'

5 *The Shadow*

I'm working in the Lucky Bar one night, or, rather, early one morning. The place is at its three o'clock peak, dancers still dancing, drinkers still talking sense. All except a big Norwegian guy causing trouble at the bar. He's talking *non* sense. This kind of talk doesn't go down well at the Lucky. They like to stay cool at the Lucky. Swaying about, knocking drinks off the counter, lurching boorishly into dancers, this bloke's becoming a problem.

The manager's son, Jimmy, is called. He walks towards the Norwegian.

'Shut yer mouth, OK? Just shut yer mouth.'

The Norseman prods Jimmy – just a little – with a fat,

son-of-toil, North Sea-weathered forefinger. It was just a little prod. But enough to upset Jimmy.

Slam, crack!

Jimmy's head makes expert contact with that of the out-of-order seaman. The sailor's eyes glaze over. He sways this way and that. Then, like a felled Norway pine, he goes down with a sprawling crash, taking two tables loaded with drink down with him.

What a mess. Drag him out, feet first, dump him outside on the step to cool off. It's 27 degrees Fahrenheit out there, so he *will* cool off.

Jimmy dusts his hands, breathes in some fresh air.

Hold on a minute, there's someone out there, murmurs a voice inside Jimmy's head. A record finishes on the juke-box, another begins. The great, mirrored sphere hanging from the bar-room ceiling continues to turn slowly. Jimmy's instincts

'There was definitely somebody *out there'*

tell him that all is now well in the club. The floor will have been mopped, trouble soon forgotten.

It's not in the club Jimmy's worried about, though. Not now. He's handled trouble a thousand times before. *Real* trouble. But there is a certain kind of trouble even Jimmy can't handle. And he's thinking there may be a spot of bother coming up right now. Outside.

'Who's there?' calls Jimmy. His voice is cracked. Purely by chance, you understand. He's not nervous. Just a little phlegm caught up in his throat. Spit it out – ptooh! Norseman still out for the count, on the pavement.

Who the hell *is* that? There's definitely *some* fucker hanging about out there.

He can just discern the silhouette of the church opposite. There's a freezing fog building up but the December sky is showing a slight greyness against the dense blackness of the buildings.

He can hear nothing, see little. Yet he knows there's some-one out there.

Then, quite suddenly, with a shock that rattles his spine, he

'It was Shadow'

realises he's staring into someone's face. Some mad bastard standing out in the centre of the street, beyond the pool of orange light leaking from the half-open door behind him.

The figure finally steps forward: Jimmy knows him of old.

The Shadow.

Jimmy's always lived and worked in Liverpool 8, yet he's never quite got used to black men. All he knew was this vague uneasiness which crept over him when confronted by those honest, know-all brown eyes. And Shadow was the worst of the lot. Gave him the creeps, no two ways about it.

'Now, fuck off, Shadow . . . you know you're barred from here – you upset me customers.'

'Don't wanna come in, Jimmy.'

A deep, gravelly voice, like a groan from the grave, at last comes back at Jimmy.

'What're you 'anging about for, then? Fuck off. You're attractin' attention to the club. Next thing, the busies'll be along, closing me down.'

This, of course, is ridiculous. There's nobody else about. And anyway, there's a man lying prone at the doorstep.

'I wanna see de artis'.'

Jimmy narrows his eyes, glares suspiciously at Shadow for a second, then backs off into the club. Slamming the door.

The kefuffle at the bar long forgotten, things have settled once more into a comfortable groove. The exotic strains of Mike Nesmith's 'Fly Down To Rio' come slinking from the juke box. A tray-carrying waitress walks quickly across the room, like a fussy hen, her bum sticking out like a shelf you could stand a pint glass on. Prostitutes are sitting about talking backslang. Scousers tend to talk quickly in any case. But when the girls are discussing clients and fees amongst themselves, they revert to this backslang, which is difficult enough for a born-and-bred Liverpudlian to understand. Foreign seamen are completely foxed by it:

'Y'alright to-nigh-ghite, babe?'

'I don't nay-go yay-get: think he's a bit fry-ghitened of

wimmer-ghimmen but he's got da mer-gunney so don't nay-go. Way-gate and see.'

Someone taps me on the shoulder as I sit sketching a couple who are glaring balefully at me through an alcoholic haze.

I turn around. It's Jimmy.

'Shadow's at the door. Wants to see you. Shall I tell him to fuck off?'

'What? Er, no. It's OK, Jim. I'll come out and speak to him when I've finished this picture.'

I've never met Shadow before. In fact, you don't 'meet' him: you gradually become *aware* of him. Walk down a midnight street, especially when the rain comes down like a silvery-black curtain, and there he is, lurking in a doorway, standing on a corner. A man with tremendous dignity, he's suffered a lot of abuse. He's known the blues, all right. A harmless giant, he's been kicked out needlessly of more places than you've ever visited. I've seen him ejected from the fashionable, cool Philharmonic for doing nothing more than attempting to sell his trinkets, toys and novelties, kept with the tatty documents and cuttings, representing his life, in a battered suitcase, which he hauls around everywhere. 'I gotta street-trader's licence,' he roared indignantly as an insensitive barman bundled him out onto the street.

I finish drawing the couple, but before I can get to the door an Icelandic sailor, built like a hump-backed whale, calls me over to draw himself and his woman. This accomplished in due course, he then asks for another picture of himself to send home to his wife. He pays me in Icelandic Kronur, which I have to change at the bar. This involves some degree of wrangling, as I don't have too much faith in Jimmy's idea of the current exchange rate. With the best will in the world, folks can get confused at this time of night.

Oh, blimey! I'd nearly forgotten. Shadow.

I hurry to the door, imagining that by now he's got fed up waiting and gone away.

But no. I peer out of a narrow crack in the barely open door. He's still there, waiting in the bitterly cold night.

'Sorry to keep you, man. What's the problem?'

Shadow shows no signs of having been inconvenienced by his long wait. Even though I'm standing on the step, he still towers above me. Freezing moisture from the fog, blown up from the river, forms diamond-dust in his woolly hair. Although his face is coal-black, I notice that the palms of his hands and the undersides of his fingers are pink. His suitcase is by his side, next to the prostrate Norwegian, who must surely be dying of exposure by now.

'Wanna talk some business,' says Shadow. 'Come to de Olympus.'

The Olympus. This is a lunatic Greek club, since closed down, on Parliament Street. Downstairs in the basement cool black men, wearing leather cowboy hats and crinkly, wire-wool beards, would play cards and smoke cigars till dawn. Upstairs, in the cabaret lounge-cum-restaurant, Greek and Cypriot seamen would come to pick up prostitutes and get me to draw romantic pictures of their plump, doe-eyed Mommas, offering me creased and blurred snapshots for reference.

I shout back to Jimmy: 'Jim, I'm going!'

'OK, John. Slam the door after you, lad.'

'I think you'd better bring this guy in off the floor, else you'll have a corpse on your hands.'

'Oh, yeah. I forgot about him.'

Shadow and I walk the couple of hundred yards to the Olympus, he striding easily, I almost trotting to keep up. We arrive at the place and walk in. A bouzouki band in the corner is playing mournful but frenetic folk-songs. Each number to me sounds like 'Zorba's Dance' played at varying speeds and in different keys.

At a given signal, just as we get inside, a Greek youth steps out onto the cabaret dance-floor, crouches down, and starts doing a peculiar, crab-like dance which involves kicking out the legs and slapping the palms of the hands onto the floor. His compatriots and their women seated at the surrounding tables clap in time and emit whoops and gargles of encouragement until he leaves the floor and another sailor takes his place. This ritual is then topped by all hands in the room slinging the dinner-plates, cups and glasses from the tables onto the dance floor, leaving the performer thrashing about in broken crockery, looking rather like a seal on a splintering ice-floe.

However, I'm not too dismayed by this performance, having seen it once or twice before. But the very first time I saw it happen, I headed smartly for the door, expecting all hell to break loose. But, casting an apprehensive glance at Costa, the surly host, I noted that he gazed impassively on the scene and I came to recognise it as a regular occurrence. At the end of an evening, the tableware is swept away and replaced.

The Shadow is often to be found here. On many a night, the club is almost empty but for Shadow, squatting in a corner, stock-taking, the contents of his suitcase laid out on a table. Flamboyantly clad Spanish dolls, Afro combs, teddy bears, Filipino jewellery and wooden barrels which can be lifted to

'Shadow and I find a quiet corner'

reveal a little hand-carved boy with a huge, hinged erection, are all hauled out endlessly from his trusty suitcase.

Tonight, Shadow and I find a quiet corner and sit down. He's never before shown much interest in my drawings whenever our paths have crossed. But now, with an air of great secrecy, he pulls forth from the recesses of his suitcase an amazing photograph. The picture shows a huge fifty-pence piece apparently balanced on its edge on the back of a lorry. At first glance, it seems perfect in every detail. Closer inspection, however, reveals that instead of the inscrutably virginal features of Britannia are the black, brooding features of The Shadow in drag, doggedly clutching a makeshift trident. For Shadow is a Carnival float designer. And, so it seems, a damn good one, too. He shows me his collection of press-cuttings, recording his successes in this field back home in Trinidad. More recently, he's won first prize several years on the trot at the annual Carnival of the Liverpool Caribbean Society, which is the only other of its kind, outside of Notting Hill, in the UK.

Shadow's latest scheme is to get an insurance company, whose adopted emblem happens to be Britannia, to sponsor his latest extravaganza. This is where I fit in. He wants me to

'Shadow waives the rules'

do some detailed drawings of the display to take with him to the insurance company's PR office, somewhere in the Midlands.

I want these drawings to be *good*,' he says solemnly as I slip the photo into my pocket. Usually, this kind of demand makes me grimace. I normally hear it from scousers, never from foreigners. Scousers always demand that I draw them the best portrait I've ever done in my life, yet always expect that I do it for half-price, or even for free. It's dangerous, if you're selling something, to even nod 'Hello' to a scouser. He'll take this as a sign that you're now bosom buddies and you'll be willing to offer your services for free to him and his (usually vast) family for evermore. But in this case, Shadow was being quite sincere and I pledged to do a good job.

Just as I was about to get up and leave, a woman, noticing Shadow, called drunkenly: 'Hey, boy! I wanna make love to you!'

Shadow, with a surprising turn of wit, replied, 'Hey, if you did, it'd be like Beauty an' 'e' Beast! An' I ain't gonna tell you which is which.'

He turned back to me and with startling frankness said, gently, 'I got dis big cock, y'know. Dey all wan' it. But none dem gon' get it. I just go home ever'night, t'ink about 'e' Carnival!'

Shadow lives alone, apparently, in a small flat in Chinatown, with only a large Alsatian dog for company. In fact, one of his common farewell salutations when leaving a club is, 'Gotta go home, now. Feed 'e' dog.'

Stepping outside, I set off walking down Princes Avenue, as usual. It's now well after four. The fog had come down so thick that it was impossible to see more than a couple of feet ahead. The pavement was slippy with treacherous black ice. My footsteps boomed eerily, the crazy acoustics caused by the fog doing strange things to sound. I was glad to get home that night: there didn't seem to be another soul on earth, let alone on Princes Avenue. Something weird was abroad, the same weirdness that had put the wind up Jimmy at the Lucky Bar.

The next night, though I'd scarcely expected it, Shadow paid me in kind for the drawings, which he seemed quite pleased with, allowing me to make a selection of gifts for my wife from his collection of combs, brushes, and bottles of perfume. However, nothing ever came of his Britannia venture, although the float itself was a resounding success, winning him yet another first prize. He'd written a polite, almost ingratiating letter of introduction to the insurance company. But this, of course, could hardly convey an impression of his fearsome appearance, and I often conjure up a mental picture of a whimpering, pasty-faced insurance broker interviewing Shadow – or 'Little Davy', as he prefers to call himself – especially when, as is his wont, the latter casually dropped into the conversation mention of voodoo and other West Indian manifestations of the occult. It seems that Shadow has what we'd call, I suppose, a *doppelgänger* or 'good fairy'. She leaps out and stops him from walking in front of buses, for example, and lends him the magic to win every Carnival in which he enters a float. This bit, at least, is undeniably true. As for his story about the time he did a Tutan-khamun float and promptly got a dose of King Tut's Curse, well – I don't know what to make of it. In the small hours, anything seems possible.

He told me all about voodoo one night and my flesh crawled. All occidental rationality went to the four winds in minutes as I sat, transfixed, while Little Davy's rolling eyes, garlic-laden breath and oft-revealed yellow teeth, like giant ivory solitaire pegs, lent emphasis to his weird stories. The night has never been the same since.

In subsequent years, I've helped Shadow out on occasions with some small detail of his often-bizarre Carnival cameos. His Quasimodo, for example, was a corker. For this, he got me to paint an impressionistic backdrop of Notre-Dame Cathedral. From God knows where he had procured a pair of medieval boots, complete with curling, spiral toes which made them look like huge snails attached to the ends of his legs. Prior to the actual Carnival, he took to clumping around the streets in these in order to break them in. For some reason, he decided that Quasimodo ought to have green hair, for which purpose he dyed a lady's wig and carried that about with him, dripping a trail of dye wherever he went.

I went along to see the finished results on the day of the Carnival. Standing on the Hope Street side of the Anglican Cathedral – a key point along the route – I peered in vain along the sedately cruising procession of colourful floats for a sighting of The Shadow. I was on the point of thinking that the whole project must have fallen through when, like a bat out of hell, along came the cab of a lorry, minus tailboard, screeching, bucking and diving at terrifying speed in between the other floats, scattering children, dogs and grinning steel-drum players in its wake. Clinging to the back of the cab, being flung wildly about, was Shadow, a clanging handbell in one hand and a weighty ball and chain attached to an ankle. He seemed to be attempting communication with his apparently demented assistant in the driving seat. He romped home to win first prize in this Carnival, principally, I think, because of the horrendous face make-up he'd used, which incorporated a real bull's eye embedded half-way up his right cheek.

Shadow is a true artist, putting artistic requirements before personal comfort, as demonstrated by the time he caused himself temporary insanity through coating his body in gold paint. He had to be rushed, raving, into hospital. A more leisurely affair was his Abraham Lincoln tableau. For this, I sat with him in the wee hours in the Somali Restaurant, sketching out ways in which Shadow's wigmaker could circumnavigate the ill-fated President's huge ears, referring to photographs of the Lincoln Memorial Statue and Mount Rushmore in one of Little Davy's library books, borrowed especially for the purpose.

I often think that some day in the future an equally perceptive Carnival float designer will devote a show-stopping display to the life and times of the legendary Shadow.

It would be a winner.

6 *One Night at Dutch Eddy's*

There's a warm breeze on the Avenue, a breeze that blows no one any good. Warm, sultry nights in this part of town can mean trouble. I'm walking to work. It's 11.30 and I'm sweating bullets already, before even setting foot in a club. I'm paranoid. I admit that – always have done; I admit to playing host to an inferiority, a superiority and a persecution complex all rolled into one. In my game, those problems can't be avoided, in fact anybody normal just doesn't get involved in *my* game. Wouldn't be normal for long, if they did. But tonight a touch of paranoia seems excusable. The tension on Princes Avenue seems, even to me, excessive tonight. I stride doggedly on towards Parliament Street, where at least the street lamps are usually in reasonable working order. Not like those on the Avenue, which is actually a boulevard, the centre strip recently restored with original, newly painted Victorian gas-lamps (not working as yet), flower-beds and garden seats. All of which is very picturesque, sure. Prince Albert would have loved it. But the crumbling houses flanking either side make for a jarring contrast.

Tramp, tramp, tramp. Marching footsteps behind me.

Oh, blimey. Here we go. Cast a furtive glance over my shoulder.

Jesus Christ. This I don't believe. Like part of an occupying army, there's a whole squadron of uniformed policemen marching in formation behind me, radios crackling. They're chatting cheerfully but purposefully among themselves. They surge past me, bobbies' boots crunching.

I turn to one walking near me.

'Not *more* trouble, tonight, is there?'

A policeman was killed accidentally last night by the driver

'The new boulevard development, Princes Avenue'

'A bus parked at an unnatural angle'

of a stolen car. Another had his nose broken in a skirmish with youths in the Granby Street area.

"Fraid so, lad.'

'Where?'

'Parly.'

'Oh, Christ. That's where I'm going.'

'I'd go another way, if I were you.'

The copper's voice floats back to me, already several yards ahead. They turn off down Parkway.

I cross by the Synagogue.

There's a bus parked at an unnatural angle up there by the Rialto, once a cinema, now an antique furniture warehouse. No lights on, but the driver frantically honking his horn. A crowd of thirty or forty youths, shouting with laughter, are rocking the bus back and forth, clambering all over it like a swarm of carnivorous ants harassing some great, dumb beast.

Then: *de-dah, de-dah, de-dah*: half a dozen police vehicles slam to a halt at the traffic lights. The kids scatter, screaming and whooping, in every direction.

One of them, a black fifteen-year-old, rushes past me, all legs and wobbly woolly hat, and whips my sketch-pad from under my arm.

'Eh. Give that back, lad!'

Instinctively using the stern, authoritative voice I acquired during part of my training as an art teacher in an anarchic Liverpool comprehensive, the assertive quality of the sound (all bluff, actually) startles even me. The lad walks sheepishly back and hands over the sketch-pad.

'Ah only wannit t'look. I t'ought it was a album.'

'OK.'

Minor incidents like this happen all the time. What *doesn't* happen all the time is what seems to be happening up there at the top end of Upper Parly. Hordes of police and adolescents, off in the distance, shouting, fighting, throwing bricks. 'RACE RIOTS SHOCK HORROR', the papers will no doubt be screaming tomorrow. But there are just as many white kids as there are black rushing to the scene.

I turn off in the opposite direction. Down the hill. Stopping at Dutch Eddy's. As it happens, the place is not really called Dutch Eddy's. It's called the Tudor Club, an elegant title which is as laughably inappropriate as the Chez-Nous door-chimes which *bing-bong* soothingly when you press the bell-push. Doing this summons forth – eventually – Archie, the beefy, laconic doorman of West Indian origin. He doesn't necessarily open the door right away: he's in no hurry – no plane to catch. Dutch Eddy himself, you rarely see. An elegantly dressed black man, his dignified, bespectacled figure is seen only as a fleeting apparition on odd occasions. He also apparently owns a club in Amsterdam and spends some time there each year.

It seems to be a quiet night, inside – up to now, anyway.

'Dutch Eddy, Archie the Doorman, and Henry the Photographer'

Quiet nights at Dutch Eddy's are quite unlike busy – or noisy –
nights. If noisy nights can be a bit on the rough-house side,
quiet nights can be surprisingly grim. But pick a happy balance
somewhere in between, and you can have a marvellous night.

Seated around a table, a small group of mature people, black
and white, are talking – disgustedly – about the fracas that
appears to be gathering strength further down the street.

'Just a bunch of silly kids – some with uniforms, some
without,' says a bulky black lady, walking to the bar.

'Yes . . . I blame the press, though. The press *and* the police.
If the police cleared off, now, everybody'd go 'ome to bed . . .
but the papers give the kids ideas . . .' A white man quaffs his
ale after this speech.

In the centre of the otherwise deserted dance-floor, a
heavily pregnant girl is doing a strangely graceful slow dance
with a jaded-looking middle-aged man with his shirt-tails
hanging out. The only music provided at the moment comes
from the seen-better-days juke box, an inevitable feature of
these old-fashioned Liverpool drinking clubs. Really, they're

ideal entertainment. Unlike the racket created by the usual modern disco sound systems, juke-box music is loud enough for dancing but not so deafening as to obliterate conversation. Also, you can select your own music instead of having it imposed upon you by some vacuous DJ exuding the kind of false *bonhomie* which is standard fare in the upmarket, downtown discothèques. Eddy's record selection is very catholic in nature: Tony Bennet rubs shoulders with contemporary reggae, Nat 'King' Cole with tastefully selected Beatles' classics, such as the macho 'She's A Woman' and the cosmic 'Strawberry Fields Forever'.

Propping up the bar is the man I call 'Cuzz'. I call him this because he calls me – and everyone else – 'Cuzz', presumably short for 'cousin'. Now, this man is amazing. Why? Because he talks in riddles. Not just now and then: all of the time. Ask him, 'How're you keeping?' and he'll reply, 'Like Knowsley Safari Park, Cuzz!'

As I decide to have a beer before starting work, Cuzz sidles up to me and with a knowing wink says: 'George Bernard Shaw – the barefooted girl singer from the Ford works in Dagenham. Ho-ho! The sky is blue . . . but so are you!'

He'll go on like this all night, uttering stream-of-consciousness, dislocated phrases one after another. A string of pearls, already.

In a corner by the bar, a gin-sodden fleabag of a woman is carrying on an animated conversation with herself. I call her the Wailing Wall because she sits with her bony, pigeon-breasted frame pressed hard up against the wall, giving forth with mind-bending shrieks and growls and long, piercing, wailing sounds. Every now and then she'll suddenly stand up, point an accusing finger into space or, worse, at you and let forth a torrent of abuse, using the most astoundingly profane language, creative in its diversity and originality.

Seated at another table is a man in his sixties wearing a trilby and a pair of horn-rimmed glasses. He has not a tooth in his head. This absence of teeth coupled with the fleshy, shapeless nose lends his countenance the appearance of the rear end of

'Ride 'em, Cowboy!'

a none-too-freshly-plucked chicken with a pair of glasses wedged onto the parson's nose as a joke. He is often to be seen drinking in the company of attractive young women. He says very little except for the one ringing phrase, 'Ride 'em, Cowboy!' – with or without an authentic-sounding, cowpoke-type 'Whoop!' at the end. This remark can be directed at anyone in the room, is repeated at intervals, and is usually followed by a benign, if toothless, smile.

Another character of similar vintage asks me to sketch him. He sports a shock of beautiful, silvery-white hair. His hooded, pale blue watery eyes stare petulantly away from one another. He takes the picture and stares at it.

'You've made me look like Dracula,' he says, grimacing at the picture and looking more like Dracula with each grimace. 'You must be suffering from depression,' he spits at me with great savagery. His breath smells like a mildewed old sock that's been dipped in stale Guinness. 'You picture artists – you're all the same –' he says this as if the club is thronged

93

nightly with artists jostling one another to sketch him '– I don't like all you picture artists. Now, me, I'm a *verbaliser* – I use *words*! I could tell you stories, make your hair curl! And I can recite *The Rime of the Ancient Mariner* and twenty-three verses of Omar Khayyám. I'm a *verbaliser*! Twenty-three verses – wanna hear it?'

I didn't want to hear it last time he asked me, and I don't want to hear it now. I slope off.

Meanwhile a young girl of about twenty has drifted into the room. I ask her if she'd like her portrait done.

'No thanks, babe. I'm not photogenic.'

'But it's not a photo, it's a sketch.'

'Well I'm not sketchogenic, either.'

'It'll be a good likeness,' I persist.

'That's what I'm afraid of . . . pity you don't do plastic surgery as well. How much d'yer charge? What? You must be jokin'. You can draw me nose for fifty pence and that's me last offer.'

Oh, well. It's always worth a try.

Dutch Eddy's is one of those places sometimes frequented by men who've just been released from prison and whose immediate needs are women and liquor. One of these types now edges up to me and says, 'I want you to do a picture of me for me Mum.' So I sketch his picture.

'Oh, that's crusty. That's fuckin' superb!' (He likes it.) 'That's fuckin' smart!'

I bask in these compliments but wonder vaguely where I've seen his face before. But then he spoils it all somewhat by adding: '. . . not like that other bastard who was in here last night. He drew me picture too and it was fuck-all like me. Made me look like a "Wanted" poster! If I see him again, I'll burst him all over this fuckin' room . . .'

Oo-er. So *that's* why his face rang a bell! I sketched his portrait only last night.

Meanwhile, things are hotting up. The Wailing Wall is in full throttle, her cries now running together in a single, high-pitched drone.

Exuberant cries of 'Ri-i-i-i-de 'em, Cowboy! Yi-hah!!' punctuate this wall of sound.

'In the beginning, there was Alice in Wonderland . . .' observes Cuzz from the bar.

'Made me look like Dracula,' says the Verbaliser to anyone who'll listen.

A smartly dressed chap calls out in cultured but inebriated tones, 'Strike 'em orf the curriculum! Strike 'em orf the jolly curriculum!'

Archie the bouncer pokes his head around the door: 'Eh! Quieten down in there – quieten down!'

I'm thinking of quitting this madhouse for the night when the ex-convict totters across to me once more. He's changed his mind about the portrait. Fishes it out from a breast-pocket. The drawing is now a tatty mess, having been folded eight or nine times down to handy shirt-pocket size.

"Ere. Take this shit back. I'm not satisfied. I want me money back.'

I slip the drawing back into my sketch-pad with a sigh of resignation, give him his money back.

Oh. Hang on. Hold everything. I'm heading for the door when in comes the band – one of the two bands which take it in turns to provide light relief – as opposed to light entertainment – at Eddy's.

Very late in arriving, the band have apparently been playing somewhere out of town. Faces already glossy with sweat, they're grunting and puffing, heaving their amplifiers up the steps and across the dance-floor onto the small raised platform which serves as a stage, elbowing away the protesting Wailing Wall as they go.

Live music! The atmosphere lightens, brightens at the prospect. In brisk, no-nonsense fashion, the musicians sling their amp-covers and drum-cases onto the staircase in the passageway and rapidly set up their equipment, chatting and grinning as they go.

'Ride 'em Cowboy' changes his tune for once. Striding up to a microphone which has just been plugged in, he announces solemnly: 'I'm in the mood for love.' He cuts a painfully comic figure: the musicians fall about laughing. The mood is changing a hundred per cent for the better.

As each of the five musicians finishes setting up his gear, he begins to play. They slide easily, one by one, into a slow but torrid blues. The sax-player honks and squeaks some smoky bar-room solo, filling the tiny club with good feeling. The drummer, last to set up his complex equipment, is finally ready and – whap! – he kicks into the groove, lifting the whole band off the ground. The entire place is now swinging from side to side. People are pouring in at the front door, Archie having to shift himself now to keep up with the flow.

The Tudor Club, like most in this area, is just the two ground-floor rooms of a once-elegant, now decaying, Victorian town-house. Glance up, and you can see the inevitable neo-rococo plaster moulding and elaborate cornices on the ceiling. The floor is vinyl. Plain, grubby, but serviceable. Easily mopped and swept. If you've ever caught the stench of stale vomit and stale beer soaked up on those plush carpets in downtown clubland, you'll know how sensible this is. Tables and stools are equally sensible and plain, if uncomfortable. Formica-topped tables are easily wiped clear of spilled drink.

By now, the band are coming to the end of a medley of Fats Domino numbers.

'. . . said, "Ah don' know why, don' know why, don' know why ah lurv yew bood ah dew!"' The gritty voice and pounding rhythm come to a stop. They're a good band. You can tell they're good because the crowd, although they will never applaud, are not throwing things at the stage.

'Right, folks!' grins the singer, 'Now – fuck me! Did I 'ear someone clap then? Or was it a frogman walking down the stairs? Now, the moment you've been waiting for, 'ere's where I 'ave a rest and you's take over! Yes, it's – (roll of drums) – 'guest singer time!'

A beaming, fat, white bloke steps up onto the stage, the band cranks once more into action. The man's mouth opens: 'Dance, dance, dance, to my ten guitars!' His voice is appallingly out of tune, but his grin is broad. Even the waitress, who's heard some bad singing in her time, has to wince. The keyboard-player struggles manfully to find the key this bloke's singing in, but can't find anything like it on the tonic scale.

The vocalist grinds excruciatingly to a halt, still beaming nodding and waving to the booing crowd, and steps down. Up steps Bertha, in his place.

Now Bertha *can* sing. A stout lady, she dwarfs even the previous guest. She used to sing semi-pro with a well-known Liverpool cabaret band called Cy Tucker and the Friars, known universally as 'Sly Fucker and the Triers'. Temperamental, some nights she refuses to sing. But tonight she's on form, shaking it. Bouncing and boogie-ing, she stridently whips through 'Sand In My Shoes'. She even gets some scattered applause.

Now she's into 'The New York Jamboree'. Melodramatic semi-spoken intro: 'Well I went into the Donkey City-eeee . . . to circumcise my donkey . . . at the New York Jamboree, in the New York Cemetery . . .' Great stuff. Then she launches into it full belt: '. . . and they was dancin' *back to back, belly to belly* . . . the bigger the woman, the fatter the ass, oh *back to back, belly to belly*, in the New York Jamboree, at the New York Cemetery . . .' And so on. You don't get entertainment like this every day: brilliant. What an atmosphere there is now! You could pick it up and cuddle it, it's so sweet.

The resident singer takes over once more. 'And now a special surprise for yer, a good friend of ours gonna do a number.' The keyboard player doodles 'Portrait of My Love' on his instrument. 'Come 'ead, John lad!'

I look around expectantly, looking for this John who's going to do a number. Realise with a sudden panic he's addressing me – I happened to mention to the band's guitarist, also named John, the other night that I used to play in a group, aeons ago. It seems he remembered this. I back away in horror.

'Er, no, er sorry, er – come off it. I haven't played for yonks . . . anyway, my fingernails need cutting . . . some other time, maybe.' But it's too late: I'm already being hoisted up behind a

microphone, sketch-pad wrested from my grip and placed carefully behind an amplifier. A guitar strap is slung over my shoulder.

I strum a tentative chord on the powerful, virile-looking electric guitar. 'Krr-r-rang!' Blimey, it sounds good – I'd forgotten how easy it is to get a good sound out of an electric guitar. All the old feeling comes welling back. Might as well have a go now I'm here. They can only throw me out. Quick, try and think of something witty to say into the mike, biding for time while I think of something I can play.

'OK, er, well . . . a lot of people think I can't draw, you know. Now I'm going to prove I can't sing, either . . .' That draws a few chuckles. 'Tell you what, "Route 66".'

Start up a chugging boogie riff. Hey, it sounds good. Good guitar, nice amp, nice sound. Inspiring. Bass and drums swing into it, like a shotgun at my back. Oh yes, this is the life . . . I'd forgotten how good it could feel.

'Well if you . . . ever plan . . . to motor west . . .' I can remember all the words, too, as an added bonus. Even the tongue-twisting middle-eight, though I have to improvise a

99

bit: '. . . Flagstaff, Arizona, not forgetting Bootle, Kingston, Boston, San Bernardino would you . . . get hip to this kindly tip . . .' I even manage a guitar solo, clanging out some Chuck Berry clichés.

Two numbers later, I step down, sweating but exhilarated. Then a sobering realisation: this is all very well, but I haven't made much dough tonight. And it's true. Fish ain't biting. Enough of this frivolity, time to start hustling again.

I slip out onto the street, slamming the door behind me. Half of Parliament Street seems to be burning down, up at the top end, by the Gladray. Thank God it's off my beaten track, anyway. They're not interested in portraits at the Gladray, which is a strip-club that once featured a notorious lady named Felicity who did idiosyncratic things with a Guinness bottle.

Heading off down the hill, I stop at the Alahram but it's so full I decide to give it a miss. Popping my head inside, I can see what looks like a sauna party going on in a coal cellar. It's like the black hole of Calcutta in there and on a hot night like tonight, well – I don't need it. I wander off into town. Stop at a very dull, very boring and polite city disco, do a couple more drawings. Slightly taken aback to see the schoolteacher of one of my sons in there. Looking a little flustered, he shakes my hand rather formally and places a pint in front of me as I sit down to sketch a giggling suburban girl, one of dozens all sporting identical Lady Diana hairstyles and gleaming toothpaste smiles.

Further into clubland, I finish up at an all-night drinking-hole, frequented mainly by Chinese gamblers, out to spend their mah-jong winnings. But I can find no more customers. At 3.45, I decide to call it a day and head for bed.

'The Croxteth, Lodge Lane'

7 Lodge Lane

To see Lodge Lane at its most typical, you go shopping down there on a Saturday. Actually, Lark Lane over by Sefton Park used to be a similar sort of place. But when they knocked down a lot of the little side streets and turned the police station into a community centre, lots of trendies moved in. Now Lark Lane is unrecognisable. Every shop which hasn't been turned into a French restaurant has been turned into a wine bar or an antique shop. It's a provincial mini-Hampstead, a *Guardian* reader's paradise.

Not so Lodge Lane. Or at least it wasn't so for a long time, though a wholefood store has ominously appeared within the last couple of years. Like neighbouring Granby Street, Lodge Lane has plenty of Arab shops and Indian shops among the very old-fashioned, small-time English grocery stores, butchers' shops, fishmongers, pet shops and greengrocers. The Arab stores are popular. Although not cheap, as everyone is quick to point out, they're open all hours. You can buy anything from a tin of cat food to a sack of coal at ten o'clock at night, if you care to. One shop I especially liked going into [so sad that so many of the *enjoyable* things about Toxteth have to be referred to in the past tense] was a shop run by a stout, gentle Pakistani by name of Mr Singh. Occasionally I'd go out at some odd hour to get cigarettes after he'd locked up. But he'd unlock all over again to let me in. Poor Mr Singh died suddenly of a heart-attack. His son subsequently took over the place, but had not much idea of how to run a shop. He soon fell foul of the law by selling cannabis over the counter. Since then, the shop has stood empty, Mr Singh's name having been torn down for some reason to reveal that of an earlier tenant, one Harry Goodchild.

So let's go shopping Saturday afternoon down Lodge Lane. On foot, of course. But watch you don't step in that heap of dog's – oh, too late. Never mind, scrape it off on the kerb. Look at all these litter bins overflowing, newspapers blowing about the place. Let's see, what do we need? Meat, groceries, fruit and veg . . .

For a start, if you've got any sense, you'll steer clear of that little Italian greengrocer. His prices are phenomenal. Look at that pineapple in the window: £2.50! Further down the Lane you can get one exactly the same for 60p. But, luckily for him, there are loads of people about with no sense. Lark Lane types, some of them: others from out in the sticks. Money no object, so it seems, or maybe they're scared of getting their cars damaged by leaving them outside the cheapo-cheapo shops further on down the Lane.

Want some meat? That can be difficult, too, if you don't want to pay through the nose. The first butcher you come to – red-faced and high blood-pressured through eating steak every day – is a great one for meteorology. Walk into the shop and, no matter what it's doing outside, he'll have plenty of

'Out shopping'

favourable things to say about the weather. Not that he ever sees any of it, locked up in the shop all day. A hot, sunny day?

'Just what the doctor ordered, this,' says the butcher.

Torrential rain?

'Just the job. Keep all that dust down. Wash it all away.' This said while wrapping some sausage, his nodding head turned towards the window, his eyes, narrowed through concentration, scanning what fraction he can see of the sky. How about a freezing cold, sleety, slushy, god-awful winter's day? Think you've got him now, don't you? No *way* have you got him. Smirks approvingly at the neo-arctic conditions:

'Ideal, this. Keeps the meat fresh and cool.'

But be careful. Don't let this joviality fool you. He's leaning on the scales!

'There we are, half a pound. Ah! Just a little over. All right with you? Lovely piece, that. Out of this world.'

Just a little over. Only 2p more, so you pay up. Who'd make a fuss over 2p? Nobody, of course. And that's what he's been banking on. Doesn't take many of those extra 2p's a day to mount up to a sizeable sum.

What's next, fruit and veg? Right. A bit further up the road you can already see the tail-end of a lengthy queue of people, mostly women, idly chatting and gootchy-gooing to wide-eyed, gurgling babies in prams parked on the pavement. There's nothing special happening here, you find, as you attach yourself to the end of the queue. It's just that this is the cheapest greengrocer's in the Lane. Sometimes you wonder if it really is the low prices which attract all these women here. In the window is a row of cucumbers, propped up diagonally against the glass, often supported by a couple of large grapefruit or somesuch. It looks like blatant phallic symbolism, but done with a kind of careless precision that makes you ashamed of yourself for thinking such a thing, Mrs Glumbody. Yet this display is always there, every day. Different cucumbers, of course, but always carefully arranged in this haphazard way. Makes you think. Could be the subject of an in-depth dissertation: 'Freud, the Sub-conscious, and the Greengrocer'. I've

'Outside the greengrocer's'

heard of stranger PhD subjects.

Twenty minutes later, when your section of the queue has crossed the threshold of the shop and you're now actually inside the place, you think you've cracked it. 'Won't be long before I'm served now' you assert smugly. Wrong again. Despite the fact that there are no less than *seven* assistants behind the counter, you could still have another ten minutes to wait, even though there may be only half a dozen or so customers inside the shop. Oops: slap-slap, tut-tut. One of the women behind the counter has just slapped a Pakistani man on the wrist for picking up an aubergine, sometimes spelt 'aborigine', and giving it an exploratory squeeze.

'Ah-ah. Don't touch,' she chides condescendingly. The offender drops the glossy, maroon-coloured object back onto the counter. Obviously this is an ancient English tradition he's neglected to observe up until now: you don't pick up and fondle your fruit and veg before buying to check that it's sound, as they do in every other goddamn country in the world: here in Merrie England you stand there like a lemon and take whatever rubbish the shopkeeper chooses to sell you. However, for a white greengrocer's, they do have rather a wide variety of stuff on display, some of it quite exotic. This is one of the advantages of living in a racially mixed community: you can get some interesting and different gastronomic delights for very reasonable prices. A varied vegetarian diet is at your fingertips and good, hot, spicy curries can be got together from the raw materials, easily available. And vegetables are so cheap, you come out of the greengrocer's loaded down with stuff that's cost you less than one grim-looking piece of brisket from the butcher's.

Bypassing the pet-shop, run by an ex-boxer with a passion for rabbits, guinea-pigs, goldfish and racing pigeons, you come upon another butcher shop run by three pleasant women who go out of their way to be helpful and cheap – in stark contrast to the Weatherman. Their sausages are 12p per pound cheaper than his and far superior.

Coming to the end of the row of shops on the left-hand side

of the Lane, after peeking in the half-open door of a kind of small factory where regimented rows of Pakistani ladies are working at sewing machines, there's nothing more ahead but the swimming baths, bingo hall and library. So we cross to the other side and work our way back down the Lane.

Stop at the little fish-shop perhaps for some ready-cooked mackerel. The man who runs the place is very pleasant, although his daughters can be a bit terse. Then maybe we can hop along to Cassidy's, the bakers, for a freshly baked, no additives, brown loaf. On the wall a sign proclaims 'Current buns, 8p each'. Thence to the Pic'n'Pay, a general and hardware store where bog-rolls and toothpaste can be obtained for approximately half the price asked in Tesco's on Smithdown Road. But excuse me a sec while I nip into this little Pakistani newsagent's for some large brown envelopes and some felt-tip pens and maybe a quick browse through his selection of second-hand paperback books.

A high-spot of any shopping excursion in Lodge Lane has got to be a trip around the Kwiksave extra-cheap supermarket. This is where you can get all the basic groceries for the week at genuine rock-bottom prices. All the stock is lying about in torn-open cardboard boxes. Specific items are difficult to find; you have to do a good deal of rummaging around. Watch you don't break your neck, skittering across the floor on a burst-open tub of margarine or a smashed bottle of disinfectant, your shopping trolley out of control, thundering dangerously towards stacked-up boxes of eggs.

If I remember rightly, when piped music was first introduced into supermarkets, the intention was to provide soft, soporific background muzak, designed to lull you into spending your money freely. At the Lodge Lane Kwiksave, they've typically but engagingly got it all wrong. Instead of harmless Ray Conniff or unobtrusive James Last, the Tannoy speakers dotted around the store boom out thunderous soul music, sometimes so loud it hurts. Young black girls standing in the check-out queue click their fingers and bump and grind to the music, making sharp 'popping' sounds with their mouths full of bubble-gum. The check-out girls themselves sit immovable, sphinx-like behind the tills, superbly phlegmatic with their deadpan scouse humour. Even when you've passed the check-out barrier, you're not quite out of the woods yet. You've still got to fight your way through a traffic-jam of empty shopping trolleys: wire-baskets on wheels, crammed together by the score, old-age pensioners standing among them looking lost, unable to find a way out of this maze.

Back on the street, we walk a little further down and drop into the Sweet Market for something to keep the kids quiet. This old-fashioned little place has boxes and boxes of sweets which you pick yourself to make up whatever mixture you want. All the different sweets to be found in a box of liquorice allsorts, for example, can be obtained here separately and, again, at impressive discounts. At Easter Egg time, the queues roll up.

Next, we bypass the Chinese chip-shop, the carpet shop, the cobbler's, and Mr Singh's old place. But I'll drop into the Arab shop for some ciggies. The name above the door shouts, in large letters: ALI 'A' MOHAMMED. The 'A' is in inverted commas, as if it's some kind of nickname. Mr Mohammed, a bald man in his fifties, is behind the counter with his pregnant young wife. And an ever-increasing tribe of aggressive infants, clambering all over the counter and shelves. Mr Mohammed flashes his gold teeth in greeting. There is Yemeni folk-music coming from a radio-cassette recorder high on a shelf.

'Twenty State Express please, Ali,' I request.

'Twenty Daily Express,' he says, scratching his head while scanning the rows of cigarette packets. I have to point out the ones I want, then there are more problems because, although I buy them every day, I can never remember exactly what price they are and Ali 'A' Mohammed doesn't have much of a clue, either. But usually his wife or one of the kids comes to the rescue.

Most of the shops in Lodge Lane have wire grilles covering the windows. However this hasn't stopped the shopfront of our last stop, the newsagent, from being smashed in several times. Fighting through the crowd of people waiting for the *Football Echo* to be delivered, thrown in bundles with a thump from the back of a delivery van, I drop in here to pay for and collect half a dozen out-of-date copies of the *Guardian*, for which I place a regular order but which I invariably forget to pick up, newspaper delivery boys being almost unknown in Liverpool 8. The few foolhardy youths who try it as a means of making a few bob for themselves generally give it up quite soon, tired of being mugged two or three times a week.

Sunday morning. Most of the shops are shut, but by no means all. I walk up to the launderette, next door to the Kwiksave, for the last time. My wife and I have finally acknowledged the Age of Technology and ordered a washing-machine. Struggling with bags of washing – no small amount with a family of five – I stop first at the newsagent to collect an armful of the *Sunday Times* and/or *Observer*, whichever is obtainable. The continuous production problems these papers seem to have ensures that almost every week one or other is unavailable, at least in Liverpool. Although I do a good deal of grousing about having to go to the launderette, it does give me the chance to plough through the papers uninterrupted for a couple of hours, though generally I read only the review sections and magazines. This peaceful reading sometimes occurs only in theory, of course. In practice, this morning there is bedlam greeting me as I push open the door of the launderette. One of the washing-machines has reneged, belching forth torrents of hot water all over the floor. Six of the eight driers are out of action. There is a lengthy queue for the Fivepenny Spin. Also, the place is packed. With mixed feelings, I realise that this is going to take some time. Within minutes a hard, tough-looking, middle-aged woman has taken it upon herself to vigorously defend my place in the queue – mainly because she's next. Lodge Lane is full of people like this, their life-worn, Brueghellian features bearing a line or a wrinkle for each dirty trick life has played on them. The women, especially, over the years suffer this dried-out, pinched, shrinkled appearance. 'Shrinkled', incidentally, is a word of my wife's invention: it perfectly describes these hollow, unmistakably northern, walnut-textured countenances.

Two and a half hours later, the washing completed, I fold up my newspapers and trudge back home, laden down with bag-wash. Tonight, I decide, I'll go for a pint. I don't work on Sundays. Not for religious reasons, but because most clubs are either shut or restricted to a twelve o'clock bar licence.

Yes, Sunday nights are generally very quiet.

'All riot on the night'

8 All Riot on the Night

There are two pubs I frequent in Lodge Lane on a Sunday night. One is the Grosvenor, a well-kept Victorian place, becoming increasingly popular with the student element billeted in the Sefton Park area. The other is the Croxteth, a rough, tough, old-fashioned Liverpool pub. Not quite spit-and-sawdust, but not far off it. It's a common sight to see red-nosed men falling out of here on a Saturday afternoon, splat onto the pavement. Tonight, I decide, it's the Croxteth. At eight o'clock I walk in. Stop to talk briefly with Alan Williams (one-time manager of the Beatles), propping up the bar, then spot a friend of mine, Louis Thomas – Welshman and artist – sitting over in a corner. I go and sit down next to him. A dedicated landscape painter, like me he's been obliged to take up teaching for financial reasons. In fact, it is the pressure of this second oldest profession which cause us to be found in the Croxteth with increasing frequency. We settle down for a quiet pint before the usual Croxteth mayhem begins: television and juke box simultaneously playing at full volume. As if this is not enough, some time during the course of the evening the licensee inevitably plugs in his electric guitar and belts out some strident Country'n'Western music. Actually, he's a good singer. Just a bit *loud*, that's all. Though admittedly he has some stiff competition from the combined forces of juke box, TV and Space Invaders machine, not to mention the raucous chatter of his regulars.

But tonight things are unusually quiet. A squat, toad-like man smoking a cigar sits heavily down near us. His trousers come up almost to his armpits, but he looks quite well-to-do, by Lodge Lane standards. Louis suddenly recognises the man as the landlord of a flat he once rented in a large house nearby and strikes up a nostalgic conversation with the fat man, inquiring after his one-time neighbours and fellow tenants in the house.

'How's Charlie, the bloke on the ground floor?' asks Louis.

'Oh, he died. Long illness, very sad,' says the man, tut-tutting into his whisky before knocking it back in a single gulp. Louis is sorry to hear this.

'Then what about the cartoonist fellow who lived in the attic?' he persists.

'Oh, terrible business. Smoking in bed, set the place on fire. Burnt to death, very sad. Cost me £2,000 in repairs.'

Silence for a moment, then Louis tries another approach.

'Then how's your dear lady wife?' he says warmly.

'She passed away, these two years since. Very sad, I still haven't got over it, you know'. The fat man shakes his head sadly and signals to the bar for another whisky.

Meanwhile, though it's almost nine o' clock, the pub is still strangely quiet. A shaft of golden summer evening sunlight slants through the window, Louis dazzled as he catches the full impact of it. He's sitting there in relative darkness, but like a Rembrandt portrait, half his face is bathed in this unreal yellow light.

The licensee strides briskly into the room, looking agitated.

'They've started. They've started again.' He's addressing the room in general. Referring to the rioting mobs who last night destroyed much of Upper Parliament Street, he goes on: '. . . I heard it at lunch-time today. Somebody told me he'd heard they were gonna do the Lane tonight. And they've started. All me bloody windows will have gone in by the mornin', the bastards. You wait and see.' Strides out again, wringing his hands.

'Don't know about you folks, but I'm staying put till closing time. They don't frighten me,' says a tough-looking bloke wearing a pair of dark glasses, doggedly ordering another pint.

'It's just like the Blitz,' chuckles an old man in a flat cap, basking no doubt in pleasant memories of camaraderie the siege atmosphere has brought flooding back.

I decide to take a look outside. Poke my head out of the front door. A lanky black youth, with a voluminous woollen tam struggling to contain his rampant, matted dreadlocks, is standing outside, balancing on a pair of roller-skates. His narrowed eyes are peering up the Lane.

'What's happening pal?' I ask, following his gaze.

'Going to be bad news tonight, lah. 'E' Windsor burnin' down all ready. Goin' to be bad trouble,' he replies, shaking his head slowly, a sense of foreboding showing in his furrowed brow. Now I can plainly see an ominous plume of violet smoke drifting up, over there behind the library, in the Windsor area. I take it that the lad is referring to the Windsor Clock, a pub frequented almost exclusively by young black people. Still looking worried, the youth goes skating off up the Lane in the direction of the smoke. Right up at the far end of the Lane, I can see there's some kind of action going on. With a start, I glance at the neighbouring off-licence and have to do a double-take. This and a couple of adjacent properties have already been boarded up in readiness. The large yard of the truck-hiring firm opposite, normally full of parked lorries, is empty. The proprietors of these firms, so it seems, must have known what was going to happen. But how?

Retreating once more into the Croxteth, I find that another art-teacher friend of ours, Mick Pidgeley, has joined our company. Although he's been in Liverpool for only eight months – an exile from Blackpool – Mick has already had his flat burgled once and his wallet stolen from under his very nose while sorting out some loose change in the chip shop. And now this. But, strangely, once back in the small parlour bay, I find there's an oddly cosy atmosphere. Another hour, a couple of pints, pass without incident. We leave at closing time: I stop to get lemonade and crisps for the kids.

Outside, it's still warm and sultry. The modest plume of purplish smoke I'd seen earlier, however, has now turned into a serious-looking column of dense black smog. The sound of distant shouting drifts across on the warm breeze. However, things are still quiet at this end of the Lane. I invite Louis and Mick back for coffee.

We find Pam and the boys tuned in to the short-wave band, finding taxi-drivers' messages coming through. Reception is very good because the taxi headquarters are only a hundred yards away at the bottom of the Lane, messages from the office coming through loud and clear, though the responses from the cab-drivers themselves, scattered about the city, cannot be heard. Although Mick is rather excited and just a wee bit scared by some of the disturbing reports coming through, Louis and I maintain an arch cynicism about it all at first. We entrench ourselves in armchairs; stubbornly begin wading through the as-yet-unread acreages of the Sunday review sections. Meanwhile, everyone else in the house is running up and down stairs, hanging out of windows, giving us regular bulletins on developments outside.

But the radio messages eventually begin to filter through to Louis and me: (crackle) *'Roger thirty-six . . . you still in Granby area . . . yeah . . . take care, lad . . .'*

This sort of fragmented talk goes on for a while. However,

'Smoke and flames over Tiber Street'

the next series of messages really makes us sit up and take notice:

'. . . *Keep away from Parly . . . riot shields . . . baton charge . . . moving into Lodge Lane, good style now . . . fall in boys . . . everybody to junction Lodge Lane/Sefton Park Road, soon as you like . . .*'

Jesus. That's us! This last message finally gets me on my feet. I hurry through to the front of the house and peer through the window. An unbelievable sight greets me. The end of our road and the entire width of Lodge Lane are jammed up with a sea of shiny black hackney-cabs, forming an impassable, honking and growling barrier. Amid much arm-waving, taxidrivers are leaning from their windows or standing about, wherever there's room, bellowing orders to each other. Excited shrieks from Pam and the boys up on the third floor cause me and the phlegmatic Louis finally to climb up there to see what's going on.

We gaze through the top landing window, aghast. A sobering sense of seeing what must be history in the making vies for supremacy with a realistic, immediate desire to panic.

Outside, the entire skyline is an angry crimson. Dense, almost tangible, banks of black smoke hang threateningly above the rooftops. The silhouette of Tiber Street School, five hundred yards away, is framed by huge tongues of green and lilac flame, licking skyward. Over there by the Anglican Cathedral is a colossal blaze, the like of which we've never seen in our lives. By its position, we guess it must be the Rialto building going up. Almost as huge is the conflagration over in Parliament Street where there is a tyre factory and a couple of petrol stations . . . Lodge Lane is enveloped in dense smoke.

Pam runs downstairs. A few minutes later I come back down to find her standing in the hall with the three boys. They've all got coats on, Pam has packed a couple of bags with her most treasured possessions. At her feet are two large baskets containing our six cats, hissing and squabbling in their annoyance at this unceremonious confinement. She's ready to evacuate, as it seems only a matter of time before the flames reach our house. Despite the desperate situation, I find myself intrigued to discover what Pam, when it comes to the crunch, treasures most and I have to look in the bags. As I suspected, they contain no material possessions whatsoever; just family photograph albums and drawings and Christmas cards made by the boys. For my part, I start mentally drawing up crazy plans to wheel my tropical fish tanks out onto the street, having visions of the poor creatures being boiled alive in a blazing inferno. But we eventually decide that the best thing to do is just sit tight. If and when the house *does* go up in flames, we've got a large back garden so we'll go out there and stay put till it's all over. Frankly I don't at all relish the idea of venturing out into the neighbourhood. There is now a complete breakdown of law and order and literally anything at all could happen . . .

It's now 2 a.m. and there's still no sign of a let-up. Louis and Mick have now given up any plans to go home for the night. We're all agreed that they'd probably get home to find smoking craters where the buildings containing their flats had stood. Louis is concerned about the fate of a large painting of a Welsh quarry he's been working on for weeks, standing unprotected on its easel in his tiny box-like bedsit. On a whim, I pick up the telephone receiver. As I thought it might be, the line is dead. We're completely at the mercy of the night.

The messages emanating from the radio become more and more surreal:

'. . . *Yellow One, where are you son? . . . Oh Jesus . . . mayday Hope Street . . . cab overturned by the Cathedral . . . they've poured petrol on it . . . driver inside . . . get down there for Christ's sake . . . police short of vehicles and men . . .'*

I make some coffee and, for some unaccountable reason, a quantity of porridge which is devoured avidly by all, sitting there in the dull glow provided by the flames outside. We've decided the best policy is to switch off all the lights, as an illuminated window might tempt someone outside to hurl something through it. But something has occurred to me which might offer a shred of hope.

All of the burning buildings I've so far been able to identify from the landing window have one thing in common: they are all business premises. It seems that the mob are directing their attentions specifically at this sort of target. Homes are being destroyed only in passing, where, for instance, they happen to be in flats situated above shops.

The bizarre radio commentary continues: '. . . *bring in more men . . . close in on the office, lads . . . mob moving towards the office . . . want a complete blockade, complete block . . . oh, Christ, I'm gonna cry in a minute . . . never seen anything like this . . . it's the Blitz all over again . . . Lodge Lane's gone, boys . . . I'm the only one in the office . . . they've done the shop next door . . .'* [that's my newsagent!] '. . . *got to get out boys . . . radio going off the air . . . might be back in a minute or two . . . going to have a look . . .'*

Silence from the radio. Back up on the landing, the view is now like a Hieronymus Bosch painting of Hell. I can clearly see the carpet shop blazing, the Trustee Savings Bank and the launderette. Monumental flames are issuing forth from the gaping window of the Kwiksave, that eccentric supermarket. On the roof of the building, small figures can be discerned dropping petrol bombs through the skylight, just to make sure nothing survives the holocaust. The fire brigade seem to have given up completely. Mass looting is taking place. Figures can be seen silhouetted against blazing shops, wheeling loaded

'Trouble-spot, Upper Parliament Street'

shopping trolleys. Others are struggling with television sets, washing machines, and fridges, probably from Duff's electrical store. It seems that the apocalypse itself is just a shot away . . . rape, murder, just a shot away. I've often wondered what the first minutes of the Third World War would be like: probably something like this, magnified a thousand times.

Downstairs, the radio crackles back into life: '. . . *Princes Park Hospital . . . geriatrics being evacuated . . . the vicar's got the mob to call a truce while they get the old folks out . . . soon as they're out, they're going in to tear the place apart . . . three hours solid looting in Lodge Lane . . . police admit they've lost control . . . Christ, they've pulled out . . . can't handle it . . .'* The gruff scouse accent continues with a litany of destruction: '. . . *twenty shop windows gone in twenty-five minutes . . . two hundred busies in hospital, I'm told . . . going in with CS gas . . . about bloody time . . . none of us are going to be the same after tonight, boys . . .'*

As the early morning sky begins to pale, we realise it's all over. True, buildings are still burning fiercely but there seems to be no further action on the streets, at least in our area. The taxi radio man's voice sounds a little calmer now. He's even resumed taking orders, phoned in by stranded travellers requiring cabs. We all agree, sitting around, very tired and stunned, that this man of the disembodied voice has got to be the unsung hero of the night.

'Aftermath'

'We ought to vote him "Radio Personality of the Year",' says Mick drily.

Round about seven o'clock, having decided it's now safe to venture onto the streets, Mick and Louis depart. I make yet more coffee but discover I've run out of cigarettes. Still running on automatic pilot, after years of conditioning, I walk out, zombie-like, to get some ciggies. I know Ali 'A' Mohammed won't be open yet, he doesn't open till ten. But I'll get some from the newsagent . . .

Walk around the corner into Lodge Lane. And then – smack! The full impact of what has taken place during the night finally hits me. The entire Lane is in smoking ruins, building after building completely gutted, every shop window smashed to smithereens. In a daze, I walk into the newsagent's. Tom, the proprietor, is walking around in circles, stunned. His place hasn't been burned down, but his entire stock and display cabinets are crushed and scattered savagely all around the shop and on the pavement. The door and window are caved in. I back out of the shop in disbelief, stepping over the debris, and walk as if in a trance down the Lane, looking for a still-functioning shop – an impossible mission, as it turns out.

The butcher is gazing, now deathly-white, at the ruins of his shopfront. He's got nothing to say about the weather today,

T.C. 81

nothing at all. Armies of policemen are about. Firemen are struggling to put out the still-blazing Kwiksave. That whole block has been reduced to a blackened shell. But the worst sight of all is the little Pakistani shop where I get the brown envelopes, the one with the second-hand paperbacks. *The shop just isn't there any more!* I've never in my life, up until now, seen a building actually burned to the ground. But this one is the first of many, all along the Lane and down Parliament Street. The other butcher's shop, run by the three women, has disappeared completely. So has the fish shop. The rest of the Lane is impassable, littered with smouldering rubble and thick, snaking firehoses, water gushing everywhere, turning the dust and ashes to mud. A policeman tells me I might as well go back. There are no shops open anywhere along the Lane, among those still standing.

Walking back, I note that despite the boarding-up precautions, the off-licence has been well-nigh obliterated. The Croxteth, however, is undamaged. Alan Geddies, the singing landlord, bleary-eyed, has been up all night with a handful of stalwart customers physically warding off the mob in order to protect his pub. I wander back home, still without cigarettes, still in a daze. I try to tell Pam what it's like but can't find the words. She comes back outside with me, this time to Granby

T.C.81

Street to see if by any slim chance there is a shop undamaged or a cigarette machine which hasn't been wrenched from its moorings. Not a chance. We've hardly gone fifty yards down the street when an apparently numbed middle-aged Indian couple come along. Everyone – black, white, brown or yellow – is wearing the same expression of blank shock. I ask the Indian gentleman if there are any shops at all open on Granby. He shakes his head gravely and walks on.

Back home, Pam decides she'll take the boys into town to do some shopping. It looks as if it's going to be a while before she can do any in Lodge Lane. Now back in working order, the phone starts ringing. It's my Dad, to make sure we're all OK. On replacing the receiver, it rings again almost immediately. A family friend, this time, Kate Reigate, artist, actress, playwright and bundle of energy. At the best of times excitable, from her flat in Catharine Street she recounts shrilly the scenes around the Lower Parliament Street end of things, describing chains of policemen, arms linked like a line of black paper dolls, others swarming into the neighbourhood like ants on a maple leaf. The Rialto and the branch of the National Westminster Bank, apparently, are still blazing.

The rest of the day passes as in a dream. Late in the afternoon I go out with my Instamatic to take some pictures. I'm working on some drawings of the neighbourhood and decide I'd better get out there quick to make a record of it all while there are still buildings remaining. The whole thing could easily erupt all over again tonight.

The hot July sun burns down cruelly on some of the worst, most appalling devastation, Liverpool has seen since the Second World War. At first, I feel a little self-conscious, almost ghoulish, at photographing other people's misfortunes. However, I feel also that, as a native, I have a stake in the area: I soon find out I needn't have had any misgivings. Parliament Street and Lodge Lane are thronged with TV cameramen and press photographers, tripping over each other to get the most dramatic pictures. Unhappily, there are more than enough awful scenes to go round, enough for the greediest voyeur among these smartly dressed, gawping intruders.

Come early evening, Mick calls round again. Though refreshed after a day's sleep, he doesn't fancy a night alone in his flat in Jermyn Street, off Granby, and accepts an offer from us to put him up for the night just in case it starts up all over again. We put the radio onto short-wave once more to find out if anything's happening.

The first sound we pick up is a strangely laconic police message. We reckon it must be a bobby with a walkie-talkie, only yards from the house: '*HQ? I've walked right up Lodge Lane and along Parliament Street There's some tension still, but no real activity as yet. Youths are congregating in the usual spots; though I was wondering, could we do this in pairs? I feel a bit vulnerable. Also, I wonder, could you order me a sausage sandwich from the canteen?*' (Crackle, fizz.)

Later, our friend the taxi man comes back on the air. Serious trouble has broken out once more but this time a little further afield: '*. . . they're at it good style on Smithdown, now . . . windows going in right, left and centre . . . the bank's gone up in Kensington – bloody hell, all me money's in there . . . youths on the rampage in Penny Lane . . . Hartington . . . Arundel . . .*'

With the combined aid of the radio and the Liverpool A–Z manual, we trace the pattern of movement. The outbreaks are more scattered tonight, as far out as Allerton. But in the main they seem to be progressing slowly in the direction of Park Road and Dingle, away from us. At midnight, we decide we can safely hit the sack. It's been an unforgettable forty-eight hours.

'God's chillun on Granby Street'

9 *Granby Street Primary*

I've always liked Granby Street. I tend to use the word
'exotic' a lot when describing Liverpool 8. But nowhere is the
word more appropriate than when it is used in connection
with Granby Street. Sadly, like so many other streets in our
area, it is now a shadow of its former self: many shops have
closed down, much modern, characterless rebuilding has
taken place. Also, the 1981 riots didn't do the place much
good, although it didn't suffer quite as badly as Lodge Lane.
Has any place suffered as much as Lodge Lane?

Most of the shops in Granby are still run by Pakistanis,
Indians and Arabs, much as they ever were, with their open
doorways and strange and rare fruit and vegetables on display. None of these shops is cheap, by the way, which may

come as a surprise when you look at the run-down condition of the buildings that contain them. On the other hand, where else can you get hold of a mango or a breadfruit or a green pepper at ten o'clock on a Sunday morning or eight o' clock on a Tuesday night? Or raw spices, not yet crushed, or wonderfully strange Indian sweet-meats, all contained in old-fashioned, heavy glass jars?

There always seems to be broken glass on the ground in Granby Street. The shop-windows are all enclosed in wire-grilles, so that bricks bounce harmlessly off them. All this rubble, all this protection. Yet, even on the hottest summer day, all seems peaceful down Granby. Families of a variety of races stroll unhurriedly around the shops. Jamaican children, already sporting bizarre dreadlocks, play in the gutter. Frizzy-haired, sharply dressed adolescents bop and boogie at the nearby Methodist church hall youth club or lounge about outside under Arthur Dooley's idiosyncratic *Christ on the Cross* sculpture on the corner of Mulgrave Street. There's not a lot for the kids to do around here, but they make the most of what's available. The older ones do their boogieing down at the Windsor Clock on Kingsley Road, where there's commonly a band or a disco playing. Not just teenagers in here, either. Some venerable old black men can be found here, too, hip as the next man, sitting there clicking their fingers, shaking their heads, hand-jiving to the reggae and soul. There's no such thing as a generation gap here, no such thing as too old to roll or too pooped to pop. Put on 'Freak Out' or 'September' or 'Superstition' and watch them go.

As I said, I like Granby. So you can imagine how pleased I was the day they sent me to teach art for a few weeks at Granby Street Primary. The other student teacher they sent along with me was Linda Jowers, a bright-eyed, laughing young Scot. She couldn't believe Granby Street itself – 'It's just like being in a foreign country' – but for her, as for me, that brief period at Granby Street Primary was magical. Of all the kids in the school, less than a third were white. The other two-thirds were black, olive, yellow or something in between. And what beautiful, open, affectionate kids they were. Many came from backgrounds of the most monstrous deprivation – Dad's in prison, Mother's on the game, sister's on the game, brother's in Borstal. Others were more lucky: one little Somali lad, Adam, of a large, happy integrated family of six, had a Dad whose substantial seaman's wages and travel concessions took them all, lock, stock, and barrel, back to see the old folks in Somalia for the full six weeks of each school summer holiday. Other kids, mainly Asiatics, whose parents were traders in Granby Street, also enjoyed a good standard of living. One Chinese boy regularly gave me a thrashing at the chessboard, my Western Yin crumbling under his relentless Eastern Yang. In a confrontation between the affective and the cognitive, cognitive ruled OK. A sad Arab boy, however, who gave me some problems in the classroom, threatened more than once to bring his Dad into school to sort me out. It was only near the end of my sojourn at the school that I learned that his Dad had left home two years previously, seeming to the

'Granby Street Primary'

confused lad to have walked straight off the edge of his small world. Miss Linda and I ran the full gamut of emotions at Granby Street, often not knowing whether to laugh or cry, feelings running so high.

A common topic in the staff room was the fate that awaited these kids when they left the ample bosoms of both Granby Street Primary and the plump, jolly Miss Hill, Headmistress. By the end of their fourth year at Granby, the kids were already toughening up. Two or three years into their comprehensive schools, many of them would become quite untameable. Some local comps, it appeared, had worse reputations than others. One lunchtime I walked into a neighbouring shop to buy a Cornish pasty. Surprised, to say the least, to find it full of curry powder, I commented on this to the shopkeeper – a large, tough-looking black man with a nasty-looking scar on his face. He turned out, as is often the case, to be another gentle giant. We fell into conversation. It seemed his daughter was among my temporary charges and I asked him which comprehensive school she'd be attending after leaving Granby. 'Paddington?' I suggested.

He looked aghast.

'Paddington? No way my girl going to Paddington. No way.'

Paddington, I thought, must be one hell of a place if this tough-looking customer recoiled at the idea of his equally tough-looking daughter being sent there.

If kids present one set of problems to a trainee art teacher, it doesn't mean that other, established teachers in the school can't sometimes present an entirely different but equally vexing set of problems. While reading George Orwell's *Decline of the English Murder and Other Essays*, I happened to come across the following quote in his discourse on Charles Dickens: 'If you hate violence and don't believe in politics, the only remedy remaining is education. Perhaps society is past praying for, but there is always hope for the individual human being, if you can catch him young enough.'

As violence and politics seemed already to me rather evident

'Young shopkeeper'

elements within the education system, I wondered whether art education had a function as a refuge within a refuge. It was difficult to imagine a useful art lesson being spawned through violence: 'Draw this delicate, fragile pot of geraniums. Else I'll thrash you to within an inch of your life.'

Ludicrous. Yet there are contradictions almost as silly as this at school. Children often troop into art lessons fresh from a violent fight in the playground or an aggressive work-out in the gym, still smelling of sweaty pumps and armpits. But now they're expected, of a sudden, to sit quietly and call upon their Muse, the better to illustrate 'A Day at the Royal Show'. This unbelievable title is suggested by one Max Dimmack in *Modern Art Education in the Primary School* as the theme for an art lesson. Imagine my suggesting *that* as a subject in Granby Street, Liverpool 8, a multiracial, underprivileged, educational priority area. Wonderful.

Orwell's 'get to the child before society gets at him' stance is a laudable but futile aim for the art specialist. But it may just be conceivable that you could get to the child before the other teachers get to him, if you're quick. Five minutes in the average school staff room can be sufficient time to convince you of the dangers that may lurk within for unsuspecting youngsters. When not reading the *Daily Mirror* or touting football club raffle tickets, non- 'art-specialist' teachers ('real' teachers) can be heard discussing what to do with an unwanted class of wayward kids.

'Give them some art!' some bright spark will suggest. Strangely enough, I'd be very reluctant to attempt to teach maths, English or science – because I'm not qualified to do so. Yet specialists in other subjects feel no reticence at all about teaching 'art'. Or, rather, handing out a few grimy boxes of paints and telling them to get on with it.

Don't misunderstand me. The staff at Granby Street were doing a great job in a very tough situation. I found them charming people: very friendly, helpful and encouraging, although they knew damn all about art. But on one or two occasions I had the opportunity of observing the workings of a non-art teacher's mind at close quarters. It wasn't a pretty sight.

I gave them a lesson on 'perspective'. Nothing marvellous or innovative: just the view from the end of their street, or a tree-lined avenue for those with more bourgeois yearnings (there were one or two). I drew a simple example on the blackboard. A terraced street zooming off towards a central vanishing point – the classic 'perspective' chestnut. Teacher strolled into the room at this juncture. Stood there for a moment, took in my drawing on the blackboard, sidled up close to me.

'That's it,' he hissed into my ear, 'show off a bit! Show 'em what you can do. Helps you to be one up on 'em. I do it with me science, y'know.'

I blinked at him, nonplussed, then turned back to the lesson. Whilst extolling the delights of movable horizons and suchlike, I gradually became aware of a strange bubbling sound, emanating from somewhere stage-left.

'Blub-a-blub, blub-blub,' it went.

Not knowing quite what to expect, I turned slowly to face the source of the sound.

It was Sir.

There was an orange plastic bucket on a side table. Teacher had his knuckles pressed whitely onto the table-top on either side of the bucket. Where do you think his head was? Got it in one. *In the bucket*. Water also was in the bucket. Hence the blub-ub-ub sound. He had a glass tube, bent into an S-shape, stuck through a cork, in his mouth.

Hello, I thought. Poor fellow, trying to drown himself in a bucket of water. He's cracked up altogether. But he hadn't. He was just 'showing off his science' to upstage me and impress the kids or to impress me and upstage the kids, I'm not sure which.

But all things considered, I did enjoy my teaching experience at Granby Street. So, I'm sure, did Miss Linda. Even more enjoyable than teaching the kids was the experience of walking slowly home in the afternoon, alongside the ample Miss Hill, surrounded by leaping and chattering kids of all nations, all talking at once and all pointing at the same time to doorways along the route shouting excitedly:

"Look, Miss! There's our 'ouse!' or 'Look, Sir! There's our dog.'

Granby Street and the neighbouring Mulgrave, Eversley and Ponsonby Streets are all too frequently written off as grimy, run-down, even dangerous, 'no-go' areas. Yet the least interesting and least inviting parts of this neighbourhood are the bits where the old buildings – and old traditions – have

been knocked down and replaced with stark new council property. Mulgrave Street and parts of Kingsley Road have become austere zones where even the outlines of the buildings take on an aggressive, harsh appearance. The well-worn phrase 'concrete jungle' is nowhere more aptly applied than here. The comparatively recently built tenement blocks are for the most part in worse shape than the older buildings they were meant to replace. Many flats are derelict and vandalised. Visitors are afraid to enter the buildings at night for fear of who or what may be lurking down an unlit passage. The remaining inhabited blocks around Coltart Street, for example, are a disgrace and an insult, not only to their hapless inhabitants, and would not be tolerated elsewhere. But the mainstream of life seems to have taken a detour around these twilight areas, tucked away in places where 'decent people' would never venture. (I'd love to meet these 'decent people'.) I wonder how long they'd stay decent if they, too, were suddenly stripped of their means of livelihood and forced to live here, under these conditions.

Not so long ago, strolling down Coltart Street, Tiber Street or Handel Street was a bit like walking through a Louisiana shanty-town. Elderly black men would sit on the steps of the run-down terraced houses – since replaced by acres of waste-

land – in the watery sunshine, smoking ganja and watching the world go by. Others would shuffle off down the street in their panama hats and two-toned shoes. Some traces of this kind of life remain in the Granby Street area, although most of the coloured folk nowadays, of course, are second- or third-generation Liverpudlians, scousers through and through, who just happen to have darker skins than most. However, it's still possible to hear a couple of the old fellows, standing on a street corner or queuing for their pension in the post office, nattering away to each other in Swahili. Younger bloods can be seen sitting in parked vehicles watching the street-life through the lenses of their inevitable dark glasses. Business is brisk at the Muslim butcher's, where the meat is probably obtained for the excellent mutton curries served up at the Somali Restaurant on Parliament Street. The Bangladesh Food Store and the Pakistan General Store are both busy, though the Cash'n'Carry, from whence the local traders obtain their dry goods, is temporarily out of action, burnt out in the riots.

The words of the song 'Obla-di, obla-da' always conjure up in my mind a colourful picture of bustling Granby Street.

'La-la how the life goes on.'

'Punters at the Alahram'

10   The Alahram

So I'm walking down Parly, wondering whether or not I should give the Alahram a try. More often than not, I go in there, whisk around in five minutes, and straight out, without doing so much as a single sketch. It does have its moments, but nine times out of ten it's not worth the bother. But my mind is made up for me by a shout from the rear.

It's an acquaintance of mine, Tony, with his girlfriend Ellen. Tony's a little fellow, five foot nothing with long hair that's greying already, though he's only about twenty-five. A great Rolling Stones fan, Tony, though he was only a youngster when he first heard them. He'd never had much family life, he was brought up in a children's home. But on one visit to his mother's place, when he was about ten, she played him a record. The record was the Rolling Stones' first LP and the first song on it was 'I'm a King Bee'. That was *it* for Tony. From then on in, whenever life got him down, he returned to the womb by playing the Rolling Stones on his tape-recorder. Say, 'How y'doing, Tony?' and he might easily reply, 'Well, I'm a King Bee . . .'

Tony's girlfriend Ellen is a lovely-looking girl. Of a white mother and a black father, she's got the warmth, the humour and the common sense of a scouser and the dusky beauty and glamour of the Tropics. Her family life wasn't all that stable, either. Her mother did the bunk years ago, leaving the old man to carry the can, look after the family. Her old man's got something wrong with his feet, some ailment that makes him stagger about like a drunkard, even though he rarely touches a drop. Consequently, he's forever being picked up on drunk and disorderly charges. It's reached the point where he's scared even to walk down the street: he daren't drink even a bottle of Guinness in front of the TV set for the reason that, if, say, he wants to nip up to the corner shop for some fags, it's odds-on favourite that there'll be a panda car passing. One whiff of ale on his breath, plus his shambling gait, and it's another night inside.

Tonight, Ellen's walking with a limp. I walk with a limp in any case, and limp back along the street to greet the pair. Tony looks a bit out of place as he's the only one who's not limping. I ask Ellen what she's done to her leg. I've been dying to ask someone this for a long time, as people ask it of me about three or four times every night. It seems Tony and Ellen have just been involved in a fracas at a club down the road. They'd entered the club with another couple who'd paid their entrance fees and also those of Tony and Ellen, who'd been walking a little behind. The doorman then got confused, as they sometimes do, and tried to charge Ellen and Tony again, for another pound each. Tony, being the sort of bloke who likes a quiet life, was all for leaving it at that, doormen not being the easiest of people to engage in meaningful discussion, and move on to another club. Being on the dole, he couldn't have afforded to pay twice. But Ellen, like a great many women, has strong principles about this sort of thing and wasn't prepared to budge. And that started the fracas. The end result was that they were both slung out onto the street, during which process Ellen lost a heel from her right shoe, snapped clean off. Hence the limp.

'Oh, there's nothing wrong with her leg,' said Tony to me. 'Here, Ell: give me your other shoe.'

She took off her good shoe and passed it to him. Tony snapped off the remaining stiletto heel.

'There you are: good as new.' Without protest, she put the shoe back on and carried on walking, this time without limping. Good as new.

'You missed your vocation, Tony,' says I. 'You should have been an orthopaedic surgeon. Doctors tried for years to do for me what you've done in ten seconds . . . what's new with you, anyhow? Did you get that council job on the parks and gardens you applied for?'

'Nah,' says Tony. 'I phoned up, two weeks after the interview, and they said: "Sorry, the vacancy's been filled. But do try again in the future." "What future?" says I and puts the phone down.'

We walk down the hill. Reaching the Alahram, I soft-soap the doorman so he'll let Tony and Ellen in without paying. They're glad to come in and have a quiet drink, out of the cold.

Most of the people in the Alahram Club are either blacks or Arabs. Seamen, a lot of them, but mostly poorly paid deck-hands and the like, not in the same class as the types who used to frequent the Lucky Bar. Ellen and Tony safely installed in a secluded corner, I try to drum up some trade.

First chap I approach is a stout black man who has plenty to say, in a loud voice.

'You wanna draw my picture? No *way* can you draw *my* picture. You'll never be able to draw *my* face. How much you charge? Well, man, I tell you what. You can have a go at drawin' *my* picture! But I tell you this, ras-clat, if it don't look like *me*, boy, not only I ain't gonna pay you *nothin*! but you better head for the *hills*, boy, because if I sit here and *pose* for you and yo' picture is no good, I'll get pretty upset because you made a *fool* out of me! Now go 'head.'

The customer is always right. Don't ever forget that.

I sit down meekly in front of this man, taking care not to occupy airspace that someone else, more important than me, could occupy to better advantage. I cross my legs and open my sketch-pad at a clean page. My client assembles his fat, black features into a menacing leer which I presume is meant to be a smile. I start sketching.

I'll tell you something. People often ask me how I do these sketches. And the disappointing answer from me is, 'I don't know.' Because if I knew exactly how I did them, as if to a formula, I'd use exactly the same formula every time. Perfect results every time. But, unfortunately, I *don't* have a formula. And if I produce a real humdinger of a drawing, a real good one, it's just as much of a relief and a surprise to me as it is to the sitter. So, from the first stroke I make to the moment when I show my client his picture, the whole thing is in the lap of the gods.

Now don't get me wrong: I can *draw* OK. Stick a teapot or a bowl of flowers in front of me and I'll draw it for you. Technically speaking, I'm an OK draughtsman. I can get everything in the right place, do a pretty accurate representation of what's in front of me, no bother. That may not be what art's all about, but it's what the man in the street wants. However, to do a recognisable portrait in ten minutes or so is a different matter, very different to just drawing a bowl of flowers. For example, I can draw someone's face, accurate as you like, everything in the right place – eyes the right distance apart, nose the right length, mouth the right shape – but damn me if it looks anything like the sitter. You can drive yourself barmy this way. It's *right*, you keep on telling yourself. It's a good drawing. All of the visual information in front of me has been reproduced faithfully on this here sheet of paper. But show it to the customer and he says, 'That's not me,' and, damn it, nine times out of ten he's right. It *doesn't* look like him, even though you can't, to save your life, put your finger on exactly what's wrong with it.

You'd think absolute concentration would be the name of the game, wouldn't you? Well, you'd be wrong. In fact, if you said that, I'd say, 'Don't make me laugh!' in rather bitter tones. Absolute concentration? In that sultry half-light, with that brain-rattling disco blaring? Absolute concentration while the sitter can hardly be seen in the gloom and in any case he's writhing around like a bag of cockroaches? Like I said, don't make me laugh. You won't believe this, but when I'm drawing someone in a club, late at night, my mind is often on anything but the matter in hand. Quite often I'm time-travelling – many years back in some cases. Thoughts come flooding into my mind: incidents from the past, even from childhood, come drifting in uninvited. Seemingly meaningless, unconnected thoughts. An example is when I was about eight years old, one day I happened to be reading a book about Aladdin and his lamp. While I was reading it, my aunt from Scotland came to visit my mother. And that's it: that's the story. Little insignificant things drift into my mind like that, and out again. Funnily enough, the same thing used to happen when I played in rock bands. There I'd be, standing on a stage in front of hundreds of people, playing the guitar, singing the song, remembering all the chords and the lyrics of the song and yet doing the whole thing on automatic pilot. While I was doing all that, I'd be thinking about getting some fish and chips on the way home or watching, in total recall, a private film show in my head, an old-fashioned black-and-white movie of some minor event in my past. Crazy . . . sometimes it's almost total regression . . .

A funny thing happens to some of my sitters when I'm drawing them. Don't forget, unlike me, they've been doing some hard drinking for quite a number of hours. And you know what happens if you sit still when you're drunk. You either feel sick or you fall asleep. You can drink as much as you like if you're chatting with people in animated fashion, or you're up

143

and about doing something physical like dancing or having a fight. But sit still in one particular spot, while you're being sketched, and it wouldn't surprise me in the least if you started to feel quite ill. Being quite experienced in this sort of thing by now, I can usually tell when it's going to happen. The eyes of the sitter glaze over. He nods his head a bit, and more often than not a silly smile appears on his face. That's the time to move out of the way. On one occasion, I was too slow in moving and this bloke puked all over my feet, just as I was signing his picture with a flourish.

When they fall asleep, it's not so bad. At least they keep still. But then, of course, it's touch and go whether you're going to get your money or not, they're that difficult to wake up. On one memorable occasion, me boys, it was *I* who fell asleep. I'd been out till first light the previous night, then I'd done a day's work at this department store I've already told you about – or, rather, a day's aimless hanging about – then I'd come out that night to repeat the cycle. I felt pretty good – you sometimes do when you've had no sleep. It's a bit like being stoned except that it's legal. The only snag is that, sometimes, you go out like a light. And that's what I did, in the middle of drawing this grinning Arab with fuzzy hair and gleaming teeth. When I woke up a few minutes later, he'd gone. He must have gone away with an odd impression of English artists. I only hope he wasn't one of these people who have an inferiority complex about being boring. Imagine how *you'd* feel if you were having your portrait done and the artist suddenly nodded off.

Meanwhile, the drawing of the fat black man is going well – thank God. He's illuminated from the side, so one side of his face is lit up by this sombre amber light and the other side is in complete darkness. This chiaroscuro effect is quite dramatic and, more important yet, it *looks* like him. I feel that I'm over the worst: self-confidence, always a volatile commodity, returns. One of my client's friends is hanging about behind me, breathing down my neck. I often find that my customers are incapable of forming an opinion of their own: they usually need the say-so of an impartial observer to decide whether or not the portrait is any good. This time I'm in luck: his friend likes the picture.

'It's coming on OK, spar,' says the gruff voice behind me. Why do these black blokes call everyone 'spar', I wonder? Probably short for 'sparring partner'.

'Of *course* it's coming on OK,' says my client, relieved that he's not being made to look foolish by an incompetent artist. 'Of *course* it's good. This guy knows what he's *doing*. Why do you think I asked him to do my picture? I *know* he's doing a good job. You think I'm *stupid* or something? Would I pay a guy to draw me who doesn't know what he's *doing*? I got so much faith in *this* guy, I'm gonna pay him *right now*, before I even *seen* the goddamned picture!'

So saying, he slaps the money on the table in front of me, just as I'm finishing the picture. I hand it to him, watch his eyes as they beadily survey it: sigh with relief as a broad grin creeps across the face. He likes it, bless him. Phew.

Actually, I think this bloke's just been a lucky fluke. I glance around and note that the club is what the staff call, 'Full o'

He likes it, bless him'

nothin' ', which means that although the place is full of people, they're mainly locals, the majority of whom are skint, with very few affluent foreign seamen among them. I decide to take a walk upstairs to flog my wares.

Upstairs is the pool-room. There's always a sepulchral hush in here. Pool seems a pretty mindless sort of game to me, but these folks take it very seriously, frowning solemnly as they contort themselves into impossible positions around the table, their hindquarters thrusting out like the rear ends of so many pantomime horses. They half-lie across the table, jabbing the brightly coloured pool balls with the business-end of the cue while jabbing the balls of an innocent passer-by with the elbow-end. Pool must be one of the last strongholds of male chauvinism in these liberated, enlightened days: girlfriends in tow are required to sit in respectful silence during game after tedious game, contemplating the fat backsides of their men – not a pretty sight in most cases.

Art, without a doubt, has to take a back seat in the pool-

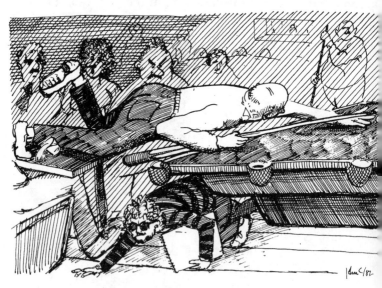

'Problems with pool'

room. But wait. A Pakistani chap, a Sikh complete with turban, is waving me across to where he sits dolefully alone. My services are required. It seems he has a son, back in Bangladesh, who's interested in art and would like to send him a portrait of his Dad as a souvenir of Merrie England – a perplexing place, full of nocturnal artists and billiard games.

'OK, just look straight at me,' I say in my usual fashion, pulling up a seat and getting my paraphernalia in order.

'Oh, no, no, no,' he says in a voice that's reminiscent of someone doing a bad impression of Peter Sellers doing an impression of an Indian gentleman. 'You must be drawing me like this, please –' He points his face skyward, as if addressing Allah. All I can see of his face now is the underside of his bushy black beard, two ear-lobes and a pair of nostrils.

'You *really* want me to draw you like that?' I ask suspiciously, wondering if he's really ready to pay for a picture of his beard and nostrils.

'Oh, yes, yes. You must in this position be drawing me.'

The customer is always right.

About four minutes later, I've completed a distinctive drawing which comprises a mass of black scribble. Somewhere up at the top centre is a parabolic shape bearing two black spots.

That's his nose, seen from a worm's point of view. I present the picture to him, not without some trepidation. But it's OK: he likes it. He's beaming at it through his whiskers. He pays me. I tread gingerly past the dangerous-looking blunt-ends of billiard cues, poised at lethal angles, and go back downstairs.

Below, tell-tale blinding blue flashes reveal that my biggest source of competition – Henry the photographer – has arrived. His business is similar to mine: he goes from club to club with his instant-picture camera taking snapshots for which he charges a fee just short of mine. Henry has the advantage over me, which is that he can whip around a room and take a dozen pictures in the time it takes me to produce one sketch.

Henry is a Jamaican, and a talented bloke. Photography is just what he does to make a few bob. Really, he's an inventor. A trained engineer, he's made some remarkable things, including the camera he's using and all its accessories. I've never seen a camera like it. It looks like an old-fashioned bellows affair but with all sorts of peculiar bits and bobs all over it, and it produces instant pictures, Polaroid-fashion. But I find Henry most noteworthy – apart from his unforgettable laugh which sounds like a lone herring-gull calling its mate – for the amazing speed with which he gets about. You can watch him taking photos at the Alahram, then leave the building while he's still at work, dash outside, catch a cab into town, rush up the steps into, say, the Cosmo Club in Seel Street, and who's the first person you see in there? Henry. Calmly strolling about taking snapshots.

Henry and I get on well, considering we're both chasing the same customers. It's an easy relationship which stems from the old days at the Lucky Bar where there was enough punters to keep both of us happy, without getting under each other's feet. Nowadays, it's different, of course. Most nights it's hardly worth the bother of coming out, business is so bad. We do it only through a combination of habit and desperation. Henry, too, has a large family to support. Being a black man, it's well-nigh impossible for him to get a job in Liverpool, where even whites are having great difficulty, so he ekes out a living during the day by doing odd jobs for people and trying to patent his latest brainwave. I've never been one for clichés, but 'necessity is the mother of invention' is one that suits Henry's style down to the ground.

I do one more sketch before leaving. A double one this time, a man and a woman. But the man's got a scouse accent, which is always a bad sign. It takes a while to complete the drawing, about twice as long as usual. I do the bloke first, then the girl. While drawing the girl, I'm vaguely aware that the bloke has gone off somewhere, to the bar or to the toilet maybe. He's taking a hell of a long time, whatever he's doing. I finish the drawing and wait patiently for his return. I haven't been paid yet. Five minutes pass and I'm still waiting. The girl doesn't know where he's got to, either. She'd just given him a ten pound note with which to buy some drinks. I decide to do a quick tour of the gents, bar and pool-room just to make sure, but deep down, I know what's happened. I come back to the girl's table, grab the drawing and show it to one of the door-men.

'Seen this bloke anywhere?'

'Yeah. He went out about ten minutes ago.'

I'd thought as much.

I return to the girl, tell her the bad news. I let her have the drawing anyway, as a consolation prize. She tears off the half with her own face on it, gives the other half back to me. The half with the bloke's face on it. I screw it up into a ball and drop it into an ash-tray.

Time to go.

'The Anglican Cathedral by day'

'The Anglican Cathedral by night'

11 *Hallucination Chorus*

My relationship with the Cathedral goes back a long way, fifteen years at least. Which, even when you're past thirty, is still a sizeable chunk of time. For example, many of my first fumblings with dope, as an art student-cum-hippie, took place on sunny days in the cemetery. Though those days seem a lifetime ago, beatniks before me had done exactly the same thing when I was running around in short pants, lying about getting quietly stoned in the cemetery. And punks, 'new romantics', *et al* are today doing the same as I walk past, preoccupied with hard reality, a home-owner and 'family man'.

I could never make up my mind about the Cathedral. Whether or not I even *liked* the thing, I mean. It's certainly *big*,

you can't escape that. It's *bloody* big. The Anglican Cathedral,
I'm talking about, not the RC one. I could maybe say a few
things about the other one but that end of Hope Street doesn't
figure much in this book. Anyway, it's Liverpool 7 down
there, not 8. But my first faltering steps as a fledgeling poet
involved both Cathedrals:

> Liverpool 8 is cool blue mornings,
> Mist over Falkner Square
> Kinky Cathedrals at either end of Hope Street
> One red and phallic
> The other white and virginal.

And that's it. Brilliant, wasn't it, Sir John?

Like the cockney who's never visited the Tower of London,
I've been inside the Cathedral only once. And then only
because a friend of mine from Yorkshire (Ray Long: are you
out there, Ray? Remember me to Jane and Alexander) insisted
on having a look. We climbed up into the nave. I looked down
and the vertigo which has always plagued me had a field day.
Whoa. Nearly puked up. Further on up the tower, up the
narrow little steps, right to the top, out on the roof of the
tower. Funnily enough, up there, right at the top of the tower,
I had no vertigo, no stomach-churning sense of panic. It's so
high up there, so incredibly, enormously, gigantically high
that you no longer have any sense of height at all. Looking
down at the landscape, it's just like having a street map spread
out in front of you. This way, mile after mile of tiny monopoly
houses. That way, the river, glistening and sparkling in the
sun; the oil depots on the other side at Ellesmere Port; Bidstone
Hill. Way, way over there, painted deep blue against the pale
blue backdrop of Heaven, the Welsh mountains – Snowdonia.

As I've already mentioned, for such a big building, the
Cathedral certainly gets about. Wherever you are, it's there
somewhere, lurking in the background, sometimes in the
most impossible places. Some places where it ought to be a
tiny speck in the distance, there it is suddenly in front of you,

this giant tower dwarfing everything else for miles around. Travelling in a boat down the river, sometimes you'd swear the Cathedral was set right in the heart of the docks. There it is, somewhere between one of the sugar refineries, or whatever they are, and the Southern Hospital. You can almost see the water lapping around the flying buttresses. Yet, when you get up there on foot, you find the thing is nowhere near the bloody docks. Crazy, crazy, crazy.

During the day, the Cathedral is weird, but fairly benign. At night? Well, it fairly puts the wind up me, sometimes, I don't mind telling you. I think it's something to do with the shape of it, like a head perched on a huge pair of shoulders. Yes: that's it. It's the slavish *symmetry*, the *fearful symmetry*, of the thing that causes the problems. I *hate* walking past it at night. Walking down Parliament Street towards St James' Road, it seems to peek coquettishly over its shoulder at you as you sneak furtively past, hoping it's not looking. Walking down the bottom end of Hope Street, by Gambier Terrace, past the cemetery, is worse still. You can't escape the vast, black, malevolent silhouette of this monstrous thing rearing up out of the solid rock. As for the main entrance side, St James' Road, well, forget it. I absolutely refuse to go down there alone at night. I mean, it's downright dangerous. There's a vast expanse of desolate, derelict land in front of it, but not immediately in front of it. Immediately in front of it are these funny little side-streets and spooky doorways. I once took a short-cut through here, alone, about one o'clock one morning. I was out sketching and wanted the quickest route from the Alahram in Parliament Street to the Cosmo in Seel Street, down by where the Blue Angel used to be. And this way seemed the quickest. Never again. I knew I'd made a mistake almost as soon as I'd crossed into St James' Road.

Away from what little traffic there was about, there was deathly hush all around, the only sound being that of my footsteps.

The hush, I could have put up with. It was when it *stopped* hushing, ever so slightly, that I started to feel uneasy. All of

'Hurry quickly past, hoping it's not looking'

the nightmares and bad trips from years ago crept stealthily back into my mind.

I could hear a funny scratching, tapping sound coming first from over there, then from behind, then from just here in front, then from over there again. This went on for a few minutes. It was pitch black, don't forget. But there was a lamp up ahead. If I could just get as far as the lamp, it wouldn't be so bad . . .

Then, all of a sudden, ' – *Wuff-wuff-wuff-raff-raff-raff-wuff-wuff, snarl, spit!*' – a bloody big Alsatian, huge it was, leaped out of nowhere, bounding all around me, lashing its tail. One of those big, big, almost black Alsatians with longish fur, like the Hound of the Baskervilles.

'Raff-raff!' Oh boy, this I can do without, I thought. Just as I was deciding to whom I ought to bequeath my debts, collected works and all future royalties, prior to having my throat torn out, a tiny little man with a squeaky voice appeared as if from nowhere, swinging a dog-chain nonchalantly about his wrist.

'Oh, dear. Give you a start, did he?' squeaked the five-foot-nothing dog-handler. 'Sorry about that. But he's my protection, y'see – 'case I get mugged. G'night!'

'G-g-goodnight.'

A quivering, shaking wreck then crossed the waste-ground, clutching a sketch-pad under its arm. God help anybody with a dodgy ticker walking that way late at night. God help them.

You'd think He would help, wouldn't you, living as He does just across the street?

Flashback, 1969. Sometimes, I thought, all of this feels like it could drive me mad; at other times, all is well. The trip from home to the Art College every day is like walking from one end of a dumb-bell to the other, each end being a many-faced prism, like the eye of a fly, as I said to Joey.

It's a beautiful day, the kind of day to walk out into the street and bump into a girl you once knew, or an old friend, to exchange cigarettes, stories and hopes for the future, but it doesn't often happen that way.

So many soft, warm female bodies abroad on a day like this: so many pairs of pink corduroy trousers, well-filled. She looks good from the back, but does an about-face to reveal a death's head. A couple of civilised-looking girls, probably straight from some office or other, down in Bold Street or Church Street, lunch-break, sit eating their sandwiches on the grass in the Cathedral grounds, looking at me with curiosity. Small world. So many maybe's!

So many maybe's . . .

'The police stopped your cousin Alan and searched him,' said my mother. Yes. You wouldn't believe the things the police do . . . that little guy in the Tavern – Paul, is his name? They offered a friend of his ten quid to talk. And the other place, they coolly walked in, planted half an ounce behind the settee and then dragged the guy off . . . but this is all old hat, anyway, and none of us cares what happens to any of them as long as it's not us . . . these pushers, I feel sorry for them . . . they don't realise that we don't care, ultimately, whether there's any dope around or not. Meanwhile they build their whole lives around it, risking their sanity and their freedom

. . . freedom! What a joke, always hiding from the law, and we don't even care, poor bastards . . . I just sit here, kind of mildly hoping the acid thing works out this weekend, but if it doesn't? So what . . it'll be R.'s first time, such a talented bloke, the world at his feet . . .

'My husband was a good man. We lived in Aldershot and he was a soldier for twenty-five years. I loved him dearly. My eldest son is a very important figure in Exeter. He's fifty-three, now, with three beautiful children. I call them children, but of course they're quite grown up, too.'

The old gentleman sitting next to her was beginning to get restless, so he stood up and let his trousers slip down to his ankles. The old lady halted in her speech for a second and carried on reminiscing as the man filled his brass-coloured underpants with dry leaves, bracken and lawn mowings, then pulled them back and sat down again, riding gently back and forth on his seat . . .

It might be nice to meet Miss G., at this time of day. To meet her in the sun, by the Cathedral, instead of that end-of-the-day bus ride when there's nothing really to say to a gentle, white-faced office-girl, so pure, so kind, so confused . . .

Dog eats dog. Like I said, so what? Rushing round, talking about cars and money. We're all gonna die some day, so why worry? It's all so *boring*, that's the big thing about it. So boring . . . There's a whole eternity lying untouched in the afternoon sun. Strange to hear the old lady talk of love . . . love occupies my mind so fully these days, it can come as a shock to realise I'm surrounding myself with people who never give it a thought. There's no reason, though, why everyone should carry the world's burden. Better that it's left upon the shoulders of those able to hold it aloft. Strange, too, that I should think of love as a burden, at the same time piling more and more onto the load . . .

One of those odd things happens. A girl sits on the bench opposite me in the patch of sun behind the small chapel place. I cast my eyes around the world, making sure they meet hers, and she glances back. Then she sits with her head down and I draw her. The sketch is weird . . . the pencil won't do what I want it to do. She gets up and leaves while the marks on the paper are only half-formed, still only dreams . . . I saw her again later in Renshaw Street. Hello and smile, like old friends . . .

When is a day not a day? When it's a dream. Back again, back again. My head was bad today, this morning, but now it's OK. True, my stomach doesn't feel too good, but that's none of my affair . . . it would have been good to wake this morning and find myself stretched out on the grass, between the pink and white tulips and the yellow tulips, or in the full noontime blaze. The garden seems full of girls when it's warm, or maybe I just don't pay attention to the numbers of old men rolling cigarettes and coughing up gobs of phlegm onto the ancient flagstones. One of the girls, young and blonde, feeds the pigeons as her sweater rides up to reveal her spine, crawling like a caterpillar up her back. The pigeons eat their fill and fly off, stopping only to rest on the shoulders of a heavy-looking white tiger that has somehow found its way in. They perch there for a fleeting moment to peck the lice from his ears and are away into the velvet-green sky again . . . a gang of navvies whistle and hoot as they pass the trio of virgins – a more honest approach, I suppose, than to sit sketching them . . .

Then she appears. She approaches softly and whispering and sits down beside me, folding her wings like a butterfly . . . I think she said her name was Rebecca . . . She's a manic depressive, apparently (funny how the people you meet, who seem the nicest, kindest, most interesting, intelligent and talented, often turn out to be nuts. Are *they* wrong, or the doctors? We'll never know. If the doctors admitted that their psychiatric patients were *not* nuts after all, it would follow logically that it must be the doctors who are nuts. And they couldn't admit that, could they? Because that would mean that the society that made the doctors into doctors was also nuts . . .) and she's in a psychiatric ward in Sefton General. All they do to her there is dose her up with tablets, instead of trying to find out why she's depressive in the first place. Treating the

symptoms instead of eliminating the cause . . . she talks softly but strongly about so many things. She's obviously used to carrying herself around, but winces slightly when I give her the drawing I did yesterday. Puts it away without comment. Seems just a little disconcerted at first, because I make so few interjections. When I do, I make myself appear as negative as possible at first by talking of my disillusionment with painting but without mentioning the songwriting and the beautiful thing that's happening to me . . . she doesn't seem like a depressive to me. She's got a lot of hang-ups, sure – haven't we all? – but the rest of us don't go to the doctor about them, I suppose that's the main difference. Her hang-ups, to me, seem to be coming from outside, social and environmental, rather than inside. She has a clarity of thought and speech that belies her freak-out stories . . .

'Don't "baby" *me*, sunshine!' said the policeman as they piled P.V. and H.G.M. into their silly blue-and-white minis.

'But what have they *done*, man? What have they *done*, you bastards?'

'Any more of *that*, sonny boy, and you'll be joining them.'

161

'Just who do you think you are?' screams P.L. hysterically. 'Now then, love: move along.'

Can't understand it. P.L. and I had been out for a 'just for old times' sake' drink in O'Connor's and met P.V. and H.G.M. in there. We sailed down Church Street, all four of us on the crest of a cloud, prancing and laughing. This policeman stops us and accuses P.V. of menacing two old ladies. We hadn't even noticed the old ladies.

'The lad didn't do nothin', officer!' says one of the old ladies. Before we know it, Church Street is swarming with pandas and fuzz. They leap on H.G.M. and hit him a few times, just to show him who's boss, drag him into a car and shove P.V. into another car. P.V. opens the door on the far side and gets straight out again. They grab him by the hair, pull it till he yells blue murder and then slam him in the face for yelling. They knock him around a bit and shove him back in the car and drive off. H.G.M. does a majestic little wave through the window and P.V. does his arms-and-hands-outstretched 'like, what's happening?' raised-eyebrows expression. And off they go into the night.

Sell yourself a world. Make yourself a pearl. Shell, shell, shell. Waiting at the corner, standing on the landing, walking on the water – you do the hokey-kokey and you turn around. That's what it's all about. And wishing. And hoping. And lay off o'my blue suede shoes . . . look after yourself. Buy yourself a bike, love yourself a wife till the mountains crumble to the sea, till the rivers have all run dry . . . don't write 'em like they used to. You shake my nerves and you rattle my brain . . . goodness, gracious – great balls of dried blood.

Like I said, Liverpool she's a witch . . . my head belongs to Liverpool, dear old Liverpool town . . . P.V. always says what a shitty dump Liverpool is, but that's a clear case of bad karma coming back on him – he hates the witch, so the witch gives him a bad time, so he hates her, so she gives him a bad time . . . must be the season of the witch . . . the witch, she flows through my veins like alcoholic poisoning. The studio at the Art College is the witch's lair for now, the peak of Liverpool,

'Tools of the songwriter's trade'

rarefied and sterile, fortified against reality . . . the pigeons amble past like fat little nuns: their heads move so fast, surely they don't see a thing . . .

Anyway, P.V. and H.G.M. finished up on a drunk and disorderly charge after the pigs beating P.V. up in the cell.

Apparently he kept asking what he was being charged with and kicking the cell door, so three coppers went in there and sorted him out. His body and limbs were badly bruised and his thumb was fractured or something, so he has to wear one of those thumb-sheath things. Also he had two massive lumps on his head where they'd bashed it against the cell wall and he had to have his head X-rayed. The hospital people weren't satisfied with the result, so he's got to go again for more X-rays. The police said that he was so drunk, he did it all himself. Banged his own head on the wall and, presumably, kicked himself in the ribs. They released him and H.G.M., who came out of it relatively unscathed, at 2 a.m. Thursday morning from Copperas Hill Police Station, leaving them to walk home. P.V. went to his parents' place. His mother took advantage of his dazed condition and cut all his hair off. Might be a good thing, really: shoulder-length hair doesn't go down too well in court . . .

Sometimes one feels so helpless . . . the acid thing worked out OK. We're dropping it at S.'s place. That's S.,H.G.M., H.L.,P.V. (pending head), R., and me – 'a good cast', as H.G.M. put it. It's like being a kid again and looking forward to a pantomime or a circus or something, really exciting . . .

The weather's been very beautiful of late.

I ended up in Manchester, it seems, standing in a bus-station, a bus-shed and a large paddock (bus-shed also being best described as large). The large red buses were, some of them, standing asleep in the bus-shed, while others were standing outside in the paddock, sunning themselves or quietly grazing in twos and threes. The paddock was contained by a shiny marble wall which embraced it on three sides, the fourth side being completed by the north-west aspect of the bus-shed. The walls were as shiny as slug-skin: the surface looked as if it had been rained upon but there had been no rain for seven years or so, according to one of the conductors . . .

I was trying to get back to Liverpool but none of the buses seemed to be going there. I noticed one was marked 'Liver' and another was marked 'Pool', but none seemed to be going all the way. So I walked there. It was early morning when I finally reached Waterloo. Hugh had been with me at Manchester but seemed to have disappeared somewhere along the line, because I was alone at Waterloo. It was a beautiful morning, misty and sunny with just a little nip in the air. I shuffled through the dead leaves and met Marguerita at the corner disguised as Angela. We met with open arms, which surprised me not a little because she's not normally given to such displays of affection.

I supposed that she'd finally seen that our years of friendly conversation really meant very little. We seemed to be making love, though neither of us were equipped with the appropriate organs – it being so early – but it didn't seem to matter. Then I was a bystander, watching the couple through the mist, making love by osmosis, pressing their bodies together so close that they became joined and the juices of their systems entered the pores of their skin and they were one, like Siamese twins. I came down to find they'd gone and there was Richard with a little cannister that he was taking to his new horn-player. A needle was mentioned . . .

I walked further on and met Butch, a skinhead, who said he admired the way in which I talked my way out of fights. I was standing next to him in the queue at the tobacconist's . . .

Making it down to the sea-front, Pete turned and saw Harry, Bill and Michael walking approximately one hundred yards behind us. He ran back to greet them, but they turned out to be just three ordinary people who bore no more than a passing resemblance to our three brothers . . .

At a later date, finding myself alone again, I sat at the window and watched a small monkey making its way across the glass. I half-noticed several other monkeys from the corner of my eye but I found it just such an effort to stay upright that I couldn't really take it all in . . .

Angela discovered that her brother wasn't dead after all, but she still couldn't explain the hole in her chest. Just below her neck had appeared a hole about three inches in diameter and inside it was what appeared to be the yolk of an uncooked egg. A large black spider had crawled the length of her body and made itself at home in the hole in her chest where it now nestled upon the egg-yolk. It is a moot point whether or not it was feeding upon the yolk, but it is quite possible that it was in fact doing so. She couldn't really see properly: looking down, she could just see one leg protruding. She had a friend who promised to come around and suck the hole to withdraw the spider, but this friend was all talk: she never actually did the job for her.

For myself, I found a place to puke. This little cubicle with a toilet in it. I hung my head over it trying to spew out the thick wads of cotton-wool which had somehow got lodged in my throat. But this was made doubly difficult by a group of twelve to fourteen brightly coloured snakes which I had to avoid stepping on. Consequently, I was executing a species of soft-shoe shuffle whilst retching . . .

Lysergic acid. LSD. The Heaven and Hell drug – the Gateway to the Cosmos. The thing you won't find mentioned in Aldous Huxley or Timothy Leary is what a *joke* it can all be! It's pure lunacy! Enlightenment? Phooey. Ecstasy? Schmecstasy. It's just a great, wild, raving joke. But a joke that can turn nasty if you're just the teensiest bit unhinged. Listen to this:

We're back in 1969 again. It's the first time I've taken acid – LSD – though I've heard all about it. Bill Stevens – you met him in Chapter Two, though all names are changed to protect the guilty – brings some round. Greenish coloured powder in little cellophane packets. This particular stuff is known in the trade as 'Green Slime'. All of the different types have these silly names, mostly taken from then-popular records. Pink powder is known as 'Strawberry Fields', purple as 'Purple Haze', and so on.

We swallow the stuff without ceremony, then catch a train up to Southport, a holiday resort not far from Liverpool. The idea is to go to this disco-dance affair up at Southport School of Art, then catch the last train back to Liverpool, where there's a party we've been invited to. Or, rather, Bill's been invited and he's bringing me along. It's quite a smart party, not the sort I'd get invited to. But Bill's clever, socially. Although he's into drugs far more than I am, he looks a lot less eccentric. Wears his hair quite short, drives a car. Socially acceptable. Not like me: I'm strictly from the moon – hair half-way down my back, shades, sandals, a string of sunflower seeds around my neck.

We arrive at the Art School Dance without incident; drink a couple of pints at the bar. Nothing out of the ordinary is happening yet. We dropped the stuff at about 7.30 p.m., it's now nearly nine. Still nothing's happening. I'm beginning to think we've been ripped off yet again, sold a dud.

But then something starts happening: my right hand is vibrating, as if I'm clutching an electric drill. Then my left hand. Then something starts going *boing, boing, boing* in the pit of my stomach.

I turn to Bill.

'Hey, are you –?'

'Yeah,' he says, 'I'm getting it, too.'

I've never known anything like *this* before. I've smoked *dope* before, obviously – cannabis. But I always found it a bit of a let-down: I've never really enjoyed it. I find it anti-social. Smoking it in company, I just shut up like a clam and go off into my own introspective little bubble, only surfacing periodically to say something stupid. But this other stuff is different, this acid.

I light a cigarette. Blimey. It's wobbling all over the place. It doesn't even feel like a cigarette: it feels more like a pork sausage or a chop-suey roll. Now that I've managed to light it, I don't know what to do with it. It seems ridiculous to stick it in my mouth. I say so to Bill, and for some reason he thinks this is hilarious. And then I think it's hilarious, too. We both start laughing, fit to bust. Laughing and laughing, tears pouring from our eyes. Laughing till it aches, till it really hurts. Hey, it *does* hurt . . .

One half of me is watching, quite calmly, as the other half laughs itself stupid. It wasn't *that* bloody funny, I say sternly to

167

myself, but it's no good. I'm a gibbering wreck. Terrible pains in my chest as this laughter, this deafening, maniacal cackling, fills the whole Universe. Bill and I leaning on each other's shoulders, laughing and laughing and laughing, tears stream-ing down. Quite a crowd has gathered around us now. Strangely enough, no one else is laughing, no one at all. They're just standing there, looking.

Then, suddenly, we're outside the railway station again. How we got here, I don't know. What happened to the dance? Were we there just a few minutes ago, or was it last night? We suddenly stop laughing and become very, very, serious – deadly serious.

'Now *look*,' I hear myself saying, 'we're not going to be able to handle this. We've got to go back on the train while we can still manage it, d'you hear?'

'Yes, OK,' says Bill solemnly. 'But first we've got to get it together to buy a ticket.'

'I know, I know, I know,' I say, staring at him with the gravest of looks: 'I *know* this!'

We pull out some coins from our pockets. They immediately fly out all over the place, rolling and bouncing all over the floor. I've forgotten exactly why we need them now – all I know is, we *need* them. I can't even remember what they are any more.

'What do we want these things for, Bill?' I whisper.

'We give them to the man and he gives us a ticket. We've got to try and pick them up off the floor.'

Very carefully, we stoop down and pick up the coins, which feel like Pontefract cakes, and gather them together, jumping about in our cupped hands like Mexican jumping beans. It must take about twenty minutes for us to gather them all together. A crowd of interested bystanders is beginning to form once more.

'Keep tight hold of them,' I hiss to Bill, as if our lives depended on it. With great, exaggerated, loping strides we approach the booking office, concentrating exclusively on getting there without dropping the coins again. With a clattering, rattling cascade we pour them through the hole in the ticket office window. Bill manages to ask for two singles without making a mess of it. The man behind the window is shouting something but the words are coming out all mixed up. Eventually, two pieces of cardboard pop up in front of us.

'*This* is what we've come for,' I announce with an air of brusque importance. 'I know what *these* are. These are tickets for the train!'

The man behind the glass is staring at me – just staring.

'Come along, Bill!' I shout. (Bill's standing only about six inches away from me.) 'Here are our tickets – we can go now.'

'That's a relief,' sighs Bill with the air of a man who's just found out that he *did* post his winning Pools coupon, after all.

'Thank you very, very, much,' Bill says with great sincerity to the ticket clerk.

'Yes,' I join in. 'Thank you very, very, much indeed. *Thank you!*'

We lope off to the ticket barrier and negotiate this without mishap. At least, we can assume it's without mishap, because here are on the train. It's moving and Bill and I are sitting facing each other. Green and purple lights, from I know not where, are playing around his head. His face is moving about as if it's made of chewing-gum – his face is a lump of chewing-gum in somebody's mouth, being chomped up and down and around. He's talking to me, but he's not making any sense. We start giggling again, this time just a quiet, subdued giggling which goes on uninterrupted for about thirty minutes, until we arrive at our destination.

We alight at the right station and walk down a tree-lined street. Suddenly, we feel fine, marvellous. The trees look marvellous. The night air is like champagne. We even know where we're going – to the party! Hey, but the trees really *do* look marvellous. Look at this one, for example.

We stand there looking at this bloody tree.

The tree is surging up out of the ground. First of all, it looks like a speeded-up film of a flower growing and opening up. Then it looks like a hand. Oh, I don't like this. It looks like a hand from *Plague of the Zombies* or something, the hand of an undead corpse thrusting up out of the soil, wiggling its fingers. (This is the branches bending in the breeze.)

'Come on – I've had enough of this tree,' I say, clinging to Bill's arm. We move off, throwing apprehensive glances over our shoulders at the tree, expecting it to come dancing after us like some corny, dressed-up pantomime tree.

Somehow we find our way to the house where the party is being held. The door is opened by a Chinese girl.

'Oh, hello,' she says, 'do come in.'

We do just that. We cross the threshold and stand there in the doorway. We won't move any further.

'Why don't you come and join the party,' she's saying. Her head is pulling itself about into wondrous shapes.

'Er, no. We're fine here, thanks, just fine,' we smile.

'But I can't close the door if you stand there.'

But it doesn't matter anyway. Because the next minute we're right there, in the middle of all the fun. Standing there, rigid as statues, in the centre of this room full of people all dancing about and party-ing.

'I know what this is,' I remark to a passing stranger. 'This is a fancy-dress party.'

He stares blankly for a second. 'Well, it's not *meant* to be fancy-dress.'

'You can't kid me,' I continue, smiling expansively and wagging a forefinger. 'I can tell by those teeth you've got. Did you get them from a joke-shop?'

The bloke's teeth are naturally yellow and stumpy. A few of them are bad and blackened. To me, he looks like Bela Lugosi.

'Are you trying to be funny, pal?' he snarls. 'These are my own teeth.'

'Ho-ho, that's a clever twist,' I gurgle. 'Bringing your own teeth along – bet you win first prize!'

He looks at me strangely, then wanders off muttering, evidently deciding I'm too stupid even to be worth punching in the face. But he's carrying a glass of some attractive-looking liquid. I follow him across the room.

'What's that you've got?' I inquire pleasantly.

'Water,' he snaps.

'Can I have a taste of it?'

'Fuck off, pal. There's a tap outside in the kitchen.'

I'm puzzled. What's *that* got to do with it?

Meanwhile, Bill is heartily congratulating the hostess on the wonderful view of the moon which can be obtained by glancing out of the window.

'I bet you thought of that when you were buying the house,' he says, winking conspiratorially.

'At the party'

I've just grabbed a handful of peanuts from a saucer and am attempting to chew them up. I saunter across to join Bill and our hostess. When he's finished rattling on about the moon, I congratulate her on the strange, rubbery quality of the peanuts. But she backs away from us, frowning.

I recognise someone who looks like an old girlfriend of mine and walk across to give her a squeeze. But I squeeze a bit too hard and she lets out a piercing shriek. She feels just like a bag of feathers, soft but crunchy.

I don't know what happened next, but we were back out on the street again within minutes, in fact in no time at all. It must be still quite early because the pub across the road is still open, lights blazing. We wander in.

The place is devastated. At least, it looks that way to me. Empty cigarette-packets all over the floor, tables littered with half-full beer glasses, it looks a terrible mess.

'What's been going on here?' I ask, horror-stricken, of a passing waitress.

'What do you mean, "What's been going on?"?'

I look back and suddenly realise that everything is really quite normal. It's *normal* to have glasses of varying degrees of fullness on tables in a pub. The odd cigarette-packet on the floor is nothing to get excited about, either.

'Oh, sorry,' I apologise. 'This mess is quite normal, really, isn't it?'

She brushes me aside impatiently and walks off.

Then Bill says, 'Do you think you can get it together to go to the bar for some drinks? I don't think I can manage it without cocking it up.'

'Dead easy,' I say, rooting in my pockets. I've got a crafty plan. I haven't yet forgotten the incident at the railway station, dropping coins all over the place, so this time I pull out a pound note, stride confidently to the bar.

'Two, please,' I demand of the tired-looking barman.

'Two *what*, pal?' he says, looking even more tired.

Oh. I can't remember what you call them. Looking around, I spot a pint of bitter standing at one end of the counter, glowing and pulsating away like something that's been left behind by a UFO.

'Two of those, please,' I say in an unnaturally loud voice. A couple of ageing regulars turn idly in my direction.

'Two pints of bitter,' mutters the barman, expelling air between his teeth in a sigh of exasperation. I pay him for the beer, managing this major financial transaction in exemplary fashion. I tiptoe across to where Bill is sitting, holding the two pints out impeccably rigidly in front of me, and place them carefully down on the table.

I flop down into a seat and wipe my brow.

'Glad *that's* over,' I sigh, with the air of a Hercules who's just completed the cleansing of the Augean stables.

We sit transfixed by the two glasses of luminous golden liquid, sit gazing fondly at them for ten minutes or more, making no attempt to drink. In fact, it becomes quickly apparent that we could no more destroy these wondrous things by drinking them than fly to the moon. I hold up one pint and we gaze at it in admiration. It feels extremely heavy.

'Wow, look at that!' I exclaim loudly.

'Too much . . . incredible!' bellows Bill ecstatically.

We invite some people at a neighbouring table to come and have a look at it, this fantastic object, but no one takes up our invitation.

And suddenly, inexplicably, we're out on the street again. But not for long.

Somehow we've arrived back at my place and are looking at two steaming mugs of coffee. We know what to do with these: we're going to drink them. But we've got used to all this nonsense, now. We're perfectly in control of the situation. We recall taking some kind of drug some time ago, which is why things seem a little odd and out of sync. But this coffee, we can handle. We know that at the moment it's too hot to drink. That's how organised we are. The coffee's got to cool down before we can drink it, so we take it outside into the street. Sure enough, within seconds, it's cool enough to drink and we stroll off once more into the night, each of us contentedly walking along taking sips from a mug of coffee . . .

I'm walking, alone, up Duke Street, several hours later. The acid has now worn off. I've been walking about all night, enjoying some crazy adventures. But everything stopped abruptly when Bill and I got to the Hole-in-the-Wall café, the all-night eatery by the Pierhead. Suddenly, everything went back to normal. We had a mug of tea each and some sausage on

'Liverpool slums that look like French slums'

toast; a wash and brush-up in the gents at the bus-terminus. We thought about taking a ferry across the river and back, but decided against it. Bill said he was going home for some kip and caught an early bus.

I continue strolling up Duke Street towards the Cathedral, feeling refreshed and incredibly sharp and cleansed around the brain. It's about seven o'clock and it's a beautiful misty blue-and-gold July morning. The red sandstone of the Cathedral is burnished by the already powerful morning sun. Dew still glistens on the copper roofing, oxidised to a livid turquoise. There are extravagantly shiny cars parked around the Cathedral steps: sharply dressed middle-aged men stand about, possibly homosexuals or gangsters, keeping a strange early morning rendezvous agreement. Oddballs, whatever they are. A young couple are exercising two huge Irish wolf-hounds, feeding them from a yellow plastic bowl.

I sit on the steps, take out a cigarette, and gaze across the vista before me. Liverpool slums that look like French slums, smashed-up tenements, pubs, cranes reaching up from the docks, the doomy outline of the Southern Hospital. All is bathed in this wondrous golden light.

It's good, it's so good, just to be alive and to *know* that you're alive . . .

Of course, there were plenty of strictly legal things to do in the Cathedral grounds. I didn't catch on to them all till quite a bit later on. Things like, for instance, just sitting there, reading a book, in the sun. Or strolling through the grounds reading the epitaphs on the old grave-stones, now – rather cruelly, I often think – uprooted and stacked up all around.

There are other things, too. One of the fringe events in a Hope Street Arts Festival in recent times was a good old-fashioned poetry-reading in the Cathedral grounds: all the ageing hippies were out in force. For example, they wheeled out Adrian Henri and Andy Roberts. Adrian, considerably slimmed-down, tanned and looking much younger, reciting in time-honoured fashion – eyes closed, gently rocking back

175

'Harmless fun in the sun'

and forth; Andy, cross-legged lotus position, squatting on the grass, twanging an open-tuned, raga-style accompaniment on acoustic guitar, sheep-dog hairstyle and flowered jacket still intact, though a few grey hairs appearing here and there. He has a degree in Law – 'Something to fall back on if the music thing doesn't work out' – but he hasn't been obliged to fall back on it yet. I'm chagrined to admit that I've had to fall back on my degree on occasions. After the performance, I introduce him to my wife and the not inconsiderable family I've acquired since our paths last crossed, working together in London several years previously. We laugh about old times, share swigs on a bottle of Newcastle Brown.

All strictly legal, harmless fun in the sun. It could easily have been 1969, give or take a few wrinkles. All of the same old crowd appearing, as from cracks in the Cathedral masonry.

'A poetry session in the cemetery'

Roger McGough's there, so is Bryan Dodson, ex-Liverpool Scene drummer, now bald as a coot, but slim, healthy and in good shape these days, though tuberculosis robbed him of a few of his best years. Mike 'Arty' Hart – survivor *par excellence* – he's there too. Harvey Loyd, late of my own seminal rock band, Krabs, still around, evil as ever, still thriving rudely.

Yes, it was good. It was all good. And, what's more, it can still be good.

Life is good.